The Last Cowboy

Twilight Era of the Horseback Cowhand
1900-1940

by Jo Rainbolt

Foreword by Richard B. Roeder

American & World Geographic Publishing

Dedication

To the old-timers.

Acknowledgments

Thanks to the women: My agent Helen McGrath, editor Barbara Fifer, the cowboys' wives—Pearl, Verna, Rose, Ruby, Viola—and the daughters, Astrid Wahl Batchelder, Marjorie Ralston Walter and Carma Harwood Adamson.

Text © 1992 Jo Rainbolt
© 1992 American & World Geographic Publishing
P.O. Box 5630
Helena, Montana 59604

Library of Congress Cataloging-in-Publication Data

Rainbolt, Jo.
    The last cowboy : twilight era of the horseback cowhand, 1900-1940 / by Jo Rain-
bolt : foreword by Richard B. Roeder.
        p.   cm.
    Includes index
    ISBN 1-56037-012-2
    1. Cowboys--West (U.S.)--History--20th century.   2. West (U.S.)--Social life and
customs.   I. Title.
F596.R16   1992
978--dc20   92-1376

Contents

Foreword

by Richard B. Roeder

Writings about the cowboy are voluminous, repetitious, and often erroneous. Most writings focus on the few brief years of the open range of the 1870s and '80s and generally end with the Winter of 1886-1887. Author Jo Rainbolt, using her skills as an oral historian, addresses a usually overlooked chapter in the history of Montana cowboying by examining the experiences of a few individuals whose cowboying days spanned the years just before and after World War I, a time when large open-range operations were rapidly coming to an end and mechanization of the cattle industry had not yet gotten far.

To place these experiences in their historical context requires a brief look at how Montana's livestock industry evolved before and after the accounts of the characters of this book. Montana's livestock story had its peculiar, if not unique, aspects, but clearly it contributed to the cowboy myth, helping shape one of the most important stock characters in American popular culture—indeed one that now pervades popular culture throughout the world.

Raising livestock in Montana began as an offshoot of traffic on the Oregon and California trails in the 1850s. By the time migrants reached Fort Hall near present-day Pocatello, Idaho, their animals were trail weary; owners were willing to exchange two worn animals for a fresh one. As early as 1850, industrious individuals such as former fur trader Richard Grant drove trade animals into the valleys of southwestern Montana, where lush, virtually untouched pastures replenished them for trade the following year.

Consequently, when placer gold miners began arriving in southwestern Montana in 1863, they found beef animals at hand. Cattle often provided the means of survival when other foods ran out and miners had to live on "beef straight," as they put it, but sating the appetites of vast numbers of miners quickly depleted local herds. Cattlemen had to look elsewhere. Nelson Story's acclaimed drive of Texas steers to the Montana mines in 1866 was remarkable for its singularity as well as its daring. Cut off by Sioux Indians' determination to prevent invasion of prized hunting grounds and by the Fort Laramie Treaty of 1868, drovers from the south waited more than a decade before they could again look to Montana, and by then they were not interested in its local markets.

Those supplying the miners turned mostly to Oregon and northern California sources of supply to rebuild their herds. Increasing numbers of cattle reached Montana as demands from miners decreased while placers played out, and ranges in the mining country soon were overcrowded. Cattle owners had to search out new pastures. They turned first to the valleys of the Sun and Smith rivers. From there they spread into the upper and lower Musselshell valleys. By 1879, John T. Murphy's Montana Cattle company, the "'79" as it was known, grazed animals south of present Ryegate. By 1880, cattlemen debouched from the Musselshell into central Montana. In that year Granville Stuart established the DHS on the Fort Maginnis range, and Thomas Cruse set up the N-bar on Flatwillow Creek. James Fergus, Conrad Kohrs and Nick Bielenberg, Robert Coburn, and Henry Sieben soon followed. These Montana outfits often raised horses and sheep along with cattle. Their owners also pursued a variety of other interests such as merchandising, banking and mining.

As these local cattlemen moved into central Montana, they began to meet herds being driven north from Texas and points between. The two lines of the cattle business were different and not always compatible. Together, however, they created the 1880s cattle boom on the northern plains, and both left legacies to a Montana way of cowboying.

The legendary drives of Texas cattle made famous by Andy Adams' *Log of a Cowboy* (1903) and more recently by Larry McMurtry's *Lonesome Dove* (1985) began after the Civil War, when Texas found itself with an abundance of cattle. Enterprising individuals sought markets in supplying both railroad-building crews and Midwest communities tapped by the railroad, but such marketing locations were generally short-lived. The crowding of trails and extension of railroads constantly forced drovers to seek out new trails, pastures and railheads. Other factors also threatened the profitability of Texas drives. One was disease, especially Texas fever, which was borne by ticks carried by the cattle. Local cattle owners turned to their legislatures for help against this dreaded invasion. Even before the Civil War, legislatures in Missouri and Kansas had responded favorably to such appeals with laws against the importation of diseased Texas cattle. Subsequent laws in these and other states were more restrictive.

While Texas owners faced those problems, the line of settlement by farmers was moving steadily westward, and by 1879 they were stringing barbed wire to protect their fields, which restricted the trailing of cattle. In response, Texas drovers moved herds farther west and north. They soon learned that severe northern winters did not usually claim unsustainable losses of cattle. They also learned that the grasses of the northern ranges were peculiarly rich and suited to fattening range steers. From these observations came a new phase of the Texas cattle business. By the late 1870s and early 1880s, Texans used their home ranges for breeding grounds and moved steers to northern ranges where they were double-wintered and sold in Midwest markets as four- and five-year-olds.

Montana ranchers did not welcome the Texans. As a defensive measure, the 1885 territorial legislature passed a quarantine law against Texas fever. Differences between the two groups also surfaced over the issue of a National Cattle Trail. In the face of expanding settlement and restrictive quarantine laws, Texans sought to protect their interests by lobbying Congress to reserve from public lands a trail from Texas to Canada for cattle drives. At a National Cattlemen's convention in St. Louis in November 1884, southern interests succeeded in getting the convention to adopt a resolution memorializing Congress to establish a trail. Both in their local organizations and at the St. Louis meeting, Montana ranchers consistently opposed the cattle trail idea. In the House of Representatives, Montana's territorial delegate Joseph K. Toole vehemently opposed the proposal, which he said would result in outside cattle grazing grass right up to the front doors of Montana ranch homes.

Adding to competition was the fact that the two operations differed in various ways. Montana cattlemen ran a cow-calf breeding operation. Their cattle were shorthorns, and they regarded long-horn imports as an inferior breed of beef animals that wasted good range. Also, the Montanans sought to upgrade their herds, and to this end they invested heavily in high-quality bulls and bought good stock from the upper Midwest as well as Oregon and California. Even the Montana and Texas cowboys were noticeably different. Walt Coburn called the outsiders "a different breed of cowhand." While both had cultural tap roots in America's colonial South and more especially from Spanish tradition by way of Mexico, Montana cowboys drew their variant of dress, equipment and style of operation from California and Oregon. To be sure, the Montanans admired the Texans' ability. Coburn said they "had the cow savvy it took to make a hand in any man's country." Yet local cowboys half-way felt sorry for their Texas counterparts because they could see that Montana hands were better fed and cared for than those working for the big southern outfits.

Nevertheless, the northern and southern lines of development came together in the early 1880s to create a cattle boom on the northern plains. With the buffalo removed by white hunters (and, more likely, cattle-borne diseases) and Indians confined on ever-shrinking reservations, both local and outside cattlemen hurriedly pushed more and more animals onto the public domain to profit from the free grass as long as it lasted. In a few brief years this frenzy transformed a once virtually empty eastern Montana into an overgrazed land crowded with livestock. A combination of factors inflated the boom, which was in full swing by 1882. A growing urban market for meat, both at home and in Europe, boosted demands and prices. These expanding markets could be tapped because of new refrigeration devices and integrated railroad and packing industries.

Raising cattle to meet the demand required labor and this was supplied by the cowboy. Unlike many late nineteenth-century industries, cattle outfits seldom had to deal with shortages of help. Many young boys, such as the future cowboy artist Charles M. Russell or John R. Barrows, later the author of *Ubet,* a classic Montana cowboy book, were inspired by the romanticized cowboy of the dime novel and were eager to try their hands at the trade. While hands were plentiful, outfits had to contend with a high rate of turnover. Probably only a minority of cowhands stayed with life on the range for more than one season. Estimates of their numbers, both during and after the boom, indicate that the glamor of cowboying quickly faded.

The cowboys of the 1870s and 1880s were generally hired employees of a corporation or business partnership. They were young—some in their teens and most in their twenties and thirties. Older than that they were too stove-up to continue as hands. A few became cooks or foremen, but most moved on. Their work was hard and dangerous. They were constantly exposed to the elements, which meant being alternately hot and dry, cold and wet. Stampedes and electrical storms in the open were especially fearsome and sometimes deadly. There was no accident insurance or workmen's compensation.

The rhythm of work was dictated by the seasons. In early spring, horses had to be gathered and broken and ridden into shape for work. The spring roundup meant branding calves, tallying herds, and returning them to their home ranges. These large, cooperative efforts covered a defined roundup district and were underwritten by all who controlled ranges within the district. A single roundup boss directed and coordinated the work. After the spring roundup, cowboys moved herds to summer pastures and subsequently to winter ranges in the fall. At fall roundup, they branded calves missed in the spring and gathered bulls to feed through the winter. Animals ready for market were cut from the herds and driven to the nearest rail center, most likely Billings or Miles City, for shipment to Midwest markets.

After the fall roundup most hands were let go until preparations for the spring roundup began. Some of those kept on lived in line camps, where they tended herds and kept water holes free from ice. A few lived in the bunkhouse and did chores around the main ranch house. Most had to rustle for themselves through the winter, either by holing up in small groups or riding the grub line, which meant riding from ranch to ranch and imposing on the owner's hospitality.

When employed, the cowboy received a pay around $40 per month plus keep. Room frequently meant sleeping on the ground in the open. Board consisted of a monotonous fare of bacon, salt pork, beans, beef, dried fruit, and occasionally canned vegetables. Hands regarded canned tomatoes as a refreshing luxury. For recreation, cowboys held various horseback contests; and in the bunkhouse, cards, tall tales and practical jokes provided diversion. The infrequent stops in towns were sprees of drinking, gambling and whoring. A cowboy's daily drugs were coffee and tobacco.

Clearly, the cowboy of the late nineteenth and early twentieth centuries was among the exploited wage-earning class of the industrial revolution. But he tended not to see himself as such. Although he was a poorly paid rural worker, unlike other wage earners of the Gilded Age he worked from horseback, and that set him apart both in his own mind and in the public mind. In the face of the cattleman's power over his destiny, the cowboy's willingness to look down on those who worked on foot or in factories, combined with his own sense of independence, meant that he was unable to act collectively to better his lot. The few documented efforts at unionization failed.

The hard winter of 1886-1887 ended the more speculative aspect of the boom. The disastrous winter was not wholly unexpected. It was preceded by a drought, and overstocking the range in summer 1886 consumed what little grass there was. But cattle continued to pour in from the south and, late in the season, from the upper Midwest as well. In anticipation of trouble, some Montana cattlemen leased land in Alberta, while others made private deals of questionable legality to run their cattle on the Crow Indian Reservation in southeastern Montana. November witnessed a series of early violent storms. Alternating snows and thaws in December covered the skimpy grass with an impenetrable crust, and unusually low temperatures prevailed in January and February. March thaws revealed ranges covered with bloated and rotting carcasses. Losses varied, depending on the range district and condition of the cattle, but generally they were very heavy. Granville Stuart figured losses at sixty percent for the Fort Maginnis range. Not far away, Conrad Kohrs salvaged about 3,000 head out of a herd estimated at 35,000.

For some owners, losses were irreversible, and they sold what cattle remained and left the business. This was especially the case for large outside, speculative ventures. Others made adjustments, and in subsequent years the cattle business recovered rapidly. Access to credit was often crucial. For example, Chicago livestock broker Joseph Rosenbaum traveled to Helena, met with Montana ranchers who owed him money, and together they mapped out recovery plans. Another response to the winter 1886-1887 was a new emphasis on putting up hay, a practice some Montana ranchers had begun even before the bad winter. Owners also developed a new concern for secure land titles, either through leases or ownership, to guarantee access to sufficient range. Control of range access was aided by barbed wire. Once a bane to the long cattle drive, barbed wire was a boon to those who wanted to control both what ranges would be used and when. This could now be done more effectively and with fewer riders. It also made possible better control of breeding. As operators extended their use of barbed wire, they sometimes illegally fenced portions of the public domain. Taken together, all these adjustments can be described as ranch farming.

While the winter of 1886-1887 was partially responsible for the development of ranch farming, it did not completely end the open range. Some home-based Montana outfits hung on. Wet years and decreased grazing combined to restore the ranges. Also, Montana livestock men turned increasingly to raising sheep. From the beginning of the open-range boom, many Montana operations raised sheep as well as cattle. In 1880, the numbers of sheep were only slightly less than those of cattle. After the winter of 1886-1887, sheep numbers increased rapidly. In the last decade of the nineteenth century and first decade of the twentieth century, Montana was among the very top sheep-producing states. However, between 1910 and 1925, sheep ranching declined rapidly due to poor markets and the increased arrival of homesteaders.

For a time after the winter of 1886-1887, a few outside outfits did continue to operate on an open-range basis. For example, in 1890 O.C. Cato, Montana manager of the famous Ten In Texas (XIT), set up headquarters on Cedar Creek about 60 miles northeast of Miles City, and placed a second base near Fallon. From both centers the XIT used grass in the Big Open, as Miles City photographer L.A. Huffman called the vast area bounded by the Yellowstone, Missouri and Musselshell rivers. But the long drive was a thing of the past. Outfits like the XIT shipped in two-year-old steers by rail to embarkation points in Wyoming and Montana for a short drive to their ranges. The XIT continued to double-winter steers in Montana until losses in the bitter winter of 1906-1907, competition for range with local sheepmen, and an influx of settlers forced it to leave. In 1908, at Burns Creek north of Glendive, the XIT held its last Montana roundup. But even then a few others, such as the Scots-financed Matador Land and Cattle Company, hung on. As late as 1913, the Matador acquired a five-year lease to run cattle on the Fort Belknap Indian Reservation near the Canadian border, a range previously used for sheep. In 1928, the Matador began to withdraw from the northern ranges because the public now demanded younger beef, and grass-fattened four- and five-year-olds no longer commanded a decent market. The Matador sold its last bunch of Montana steers in 1930.

The transition from open range to ranch farming steadily changed the nature of the cowboy's work; and with the passage of each year, changes accelerated. The pace of a cowboy's life still was marked by changes in the season, by calving, branding, gathering and moving herds from winter to summer pastures and back again. But with the cattle kingdom's passing, fewer and fewer straight riding jobs were left. Line camps were a thing of the past. Men rode fence lines rather than imaginary range boundaries. And they had to dismount to repair damaged fences. The cowboy became a hay hand and repaired windmills and tended irrigation ditches. After World War I, much of this work increasingly involved motor vehicles. The chuck wagon gave way to the pickup and stock trailer. Cowboy work centered less on riding and increasingly on fixing machinery. The cowboy had to be as much a mechanic as an occasional rider. Changes marked even such old procedures as roping, with synthetic fiber catch ropes replacing those of braided rawhide, maguey fiber or manila hemp. Pasture breeding gave way to artificial insemination. Increasingly, the need for manpower was reduced by such innovations as portable corrals, branding pens, squeeze chutes and calf tables. The changes continued, until today the riding cowboy is a feedlot worker.

For a very few single cowboys today, the center of life continues to be the bunkhouse. But far more typically, today's cowboy is married, has a family he lives with, and commands time off for recreation and vacations. But the business continues to show little upward mobility. That the present-day cowboy without an inheritance or an advantageous marriage will move up to be a cattleman in his own right is even less likely than it was in the nineteenth century.

Strangely, as the heyday of the open range faded and as the trend to fewer numbers and increasing mechanization continued, the importance of the cowboy in our popular culture has continued to grow over time. Now the image of the cowboy pervades numerous interstices of American life. Indeed, he is now, clearly, a world-wide phenomenon. This popularity is all the more surprising because the cowboy initially occupied a very low rung on the social order, the open-range period was so short in duration, and so few men (perhaps as few as 30,000) actually experienced cowboying as a way of life.

Public awareness of the cowboy awakened in the late 1860s when journalists first began chronicling the lives of cowboys working the long Texas drives. However, until about the mid-1880s, decent people regarded them as ill-bred rowdies whose way of life bordered on the criminal. The term "cowboy" is a very old one, but until well into the nineteenth century it had un-flattering connotations. Generally, English-speaking peoples used the term "drover" for those who moved cattle to markets and "cow-keeper" for those who tended and raised cattle. As the center of cattle raising moved from its old colonial centers in the South to Texas, the Spanish-Mexican cattle-rais-ing tradition influenced the North Americans. Consequently, Texans for a time applied the term "vaquero" to those who handled cattle. It was not until the post–Civil War cattle drives north out of Texas that "cow-boy" became a common term, and many writers did not drop the hyphen until about 1900, when current use prevailed.

In the nineteenth century, popular opinion had a higher regard for employers than it did their employees. Late nineteenth-century Americans were dazzled by entrepreneurship, i.e., the ability to bring capital, labor and know-how together to create new enterprises. Successful managers such as Carnegie in steel, Hill in railroading, and Rockefeller in oil were popular, folk heroes. This outlook meant that initially cattlemen and bankers, the inves-tors and organizers who advanced cattle raising to a new height of business, were the real heroes of the open-range boom. In Montana, this meant respect and accolades for men who could belong to the Montana Club (Helena) or the Miles City Club, and who could build palatial town homes for their wom-enfolk and children. Even small cowtowns provided good, sometimes lavish, accommodations for local cattlemen and out-of-town brokers. The cowboy did not patronize these establishments. His wants were met by the saloon and dance hall, or combinations of both, where he could drink, gamble at cards or dice, dance, and come to terms with a prostitute.

Ranch managers often imposed rigid rules of conduct and exercised firm control over their work forces. They sometimes reduced the code to written form. The XIT, for example, gave its hands a rather lengthy document of several printed pages of "do's" and "don'ts." In general, the hired hand was expected to be scrupulously honest and cheerful, to work long hard days without complaint, and refrain from alcohol while on the job. Ranch man-agers expected cowboys to treat decent women with chivalrous respect and place them on a pedestal. Cowboys were expected to be helpful to women. (But cowboys' chivalry and respect were generally alloyed with a fear of de-cent women.) The cowboy was expected to show loyalty to his outfit and fellow workers. He was to treat his string of horses well; abuse of a horse could be grounds for firing. Other breaches of the code could be handled by shun-ning, or by the foreman's depriving him of his favorite horse, a sure sign that he had better move on. The cowboy did not have an elevated view of his sta-tion in society. Certainly he did not regard himself as romantic. He did see himself as more fortunate than eastern workers whom he regarded as victims chained to a relentless routine.

Despite the prevalence of self-made–man mythology in nineteenth century American culture, the open-range cattle industry was not a place of opportunity and upward mobility for the common man. At best some cow-punchers dreamed of a life as a saloon keeper after age made work in the saddle too difficult. Very few rose to be cattlemen in their own right. In fact, many outfits had rules against employees running their own cattle. Moreover, social discrimination was not confined to the line between cattleman and cowboy. Racial distinctions were also clear. Regionally, cowboys included significant numbers of blacks and Mexicans, and some Indians; and while all worked together, racial and color lines were always present. Probably a majority of cowboys were of southern background. In any case, they saw themselves as members of the "Anglo Saxon" race. Cowboy saloons were often segregated and Anglo cowboys stereotyped Mexicans as "greasers." This kind of prejudice was probably a factor in the cowboy's negative response to sheep herders, since they not only worked mostly on foot but frequently also were Basques or other immigrants.

While the motives among those who stuck to cowboying surely varied, probably many opted for a way of life that, for reasons known only to the individual if at all, minimized social intercourse and the requirements of social existence. While today this may seem to reveal his inadequacy as a social being, at a time when more and more workers were confined to factories and the rigid discipline of industrial life, to his contemporaries the cowboy seemed to enjoy personal freedom. If he possessed sufficient skills, he did have freedom to move from outfit to outfit. But even this could be limited by managers who blackballed workers for serious breaches of the rules, such as flirting with unionization.

The cowboy's way of life began attracting national attention at a time when the boom and trail drives were coming to an end, and the work of the cowboy was changing. He appeared as a hero first in the dime novels whose popularity stretched from post–Civil War years to about 1920. The most notable character of this medium, Deadwood Dick, appeared as early as 1884 in Beadle's Pocket Library. Dime novels were cranked out by writers who knew little about the West and used preposterous formula plots to satisfy the appetites of an unsophisticated reading public. The cowboy's stature also grew with his use on the popular stage and through demonstrations of riding and shooting skills in Wild West shows.

In the 1880s, Rufus Zogbaum began using the cowboy for illustrations in such prestigious periodicals as *Harper's Weekly*. Zogbaum's illustrations were soon joined by those of Frederick Remington, a representative of the eastern cultural establishment, and then by a real cowboy illustrator, Charles M. Russell. Two other figures of the eastern establishment, Theodore Roosevelt and Owen Wister, added luster to the cowboy's image. Roosevelt's reminiscences of western ranch life added an aura of respectability and his "Rough Riders" a heroic dimension. In respectable fiction, Wister raised the cowboy to a new level when he published *The Virginian* (1902). In 1904, Bertha Muzzy, a school teacher from Big Sandy, Montana writing under the name B.M. Bower, began adding to the popularity of the cowboy story when she produced the first of more than sixty novels, *Chip of the Flying U,* with illustrations by Russell.

With the western story now established, pulp fiction replaced the dime novel by the 1920s. Some pulp writers, such as Montana's Walt Coburn, were real story tellers who had first-hand familiarity with the West. Illustrations by such noteworthies as Nick Eggenhofer and N.C. Wyeth often accompanied the pulp stories. While the pulps were a step or two above the dime novels, their cowboy heroes were not really working hands but men of action whose exploits had little do to with the realities of the cowboy's life. In the field of popular but respectable literature, Zane Grey added to the cowboy's popularity and gave him a much wider audience than had the pulps. This tradition culminated with Louis L'Amour, the most successful writer of popular westerns in U.S. history, as anyone who has been to a supermarket, drug store or airport can attest.

With the cowboy's image fixed securely in popular culture by the written word, his image has been successively exploited by movies, radio and teLevi'sion. In the process, his attributes have undergone changes. Early movies showed him to be an acrobatic, daredevil rider, much as he had been in the Wild West shows. The daredevil was followed by the crooner with the slick clean image of Gene Autry and Roy Rogers. Most recently, teLevi'sion portrayed him as a non-working, fun-loving he-man to sell tobacco products, beer and men's cologne.

Whatever the medium, the twentieth-century cowboy has become a symbol of manly, courageous and rugged individualism—a symbol of the lost innocence of the frontier spirit of America. As such, he has satisfied the yearning for a simpler time when it was easy to know the good guys from the bad, and the former always beat the latter.

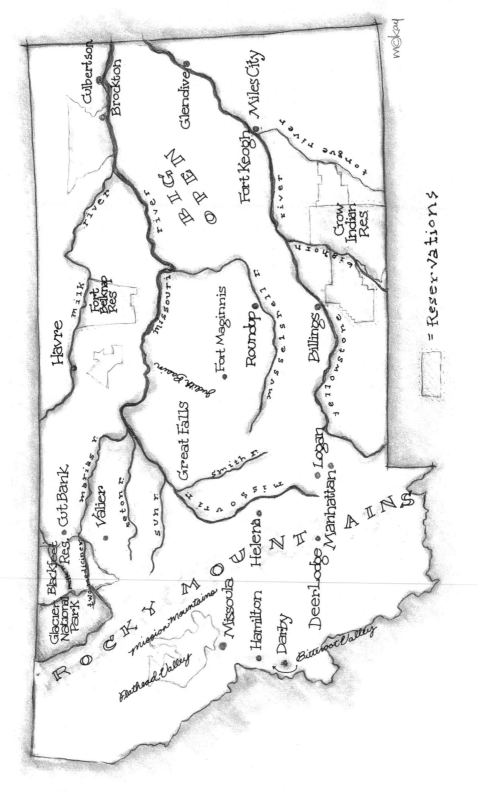

The Cowboys

Tony Grace. Born in Milwaukee June 10, 1890. Worked his way west on the railroad at age 17 to learn what he calls the business of being a cowhand. Retired at 90 from ranching in Wyoming and Montana to the logging town of Darby, Montana. Moved twenty miles north to a retirement home in Hamilton at age 101 when his wife Viola died in 1990.

Joe Hughes. Born September 7, 1893 northeast of Hamilton, where his Irish father was copper king Marcus Daly's gardener and ranch manager. Settled on a small ranch in the same area with his wife Pearl after sowing his wild oats as a working cowhand in eastern Montana. Died in Hamilton January 31, 1984.

Art Wahl. Born December 20, 1891 in Honefoss (translated "Chicken Falls"), Norway. Came to the United States at age 14 to become a cowboy. Worked as a cowhand until age 40, when he settled down with Borghild ("Bert"), a girl from home. Died in the Columbia Falls (Montana) Veterans Home, April 12, 1991.

J.K. Ralston. Born into a Montana pioneer family in Choteau, March 31, 1896. Put his early experiences as a cowhand into paintings to became a prominent Western artist. He and his wife Willo settled in Billings to raised their family. Died in Billings November 26, 1987.

Kenny Trowbridge. Born August 27, 1912 in Webster City, Iowa. Followed his chuck wagon cook father west as a kid. He and his wife Verna lived in the remote Lemhi Valley in Idaho, where the old-style methods of cowherding were still used, until 1942 when they settled in Darby, Montana. Died August 28, 1989.

Tom Harwood. Born July 26, 1900, on Shonkin Creek near Fort Benton, Montana, descendant of early Scottish explorer and Blackfeet chief. Raised horses and ranched in Cut Bank–Valier country in northwestern Montana. Shortly after he died on February 1, 1989, the ranch where he and his wife Ruby lived and raised their family burned to the ground in the middle of the night. Ruby got Tom's beloved fiddle out from under the bed, but that was it.

Donovan McGee. Born June 10, 1908, in Buffalo Springs, Clay Country, Texas. Moved at age six to Wyoming. Grew up (fatherless) with old cowhands like his uncle Sam Aldrich (Big Elk Absorkee Sam to the Shoshone), who ranched until he was 90 on his spread adjacent to Buffalo Bill's ranch near Cody, Wyoming. Don traded his spurs for a fishing boat and lives with his wife, Rose, in Juneau, Alaska.

Their Land

Montanans are like rivals in cow camps, or hometown football fans—which side is best? Western Montana, the heavily glaciated mountainous part of the state, with craggy peaks, deep valleys and more temperate weather? Or eastern Montana with endless plains, big sky sunsets and record winter storms? Being partial to living in the midst of mountains, I'd dismissed Montana's plains as that-flatland-over-east. Not so, said Tony Grace. "Miles City," he said, "isn't exactly flat or exactly rough. North of Miles you find rolling grass—buffalo was the main grass, good quality—and south are badlands, what we called gumbo, mostly clay. There's rivers, buttes—it's not flat country. The washups [gullies] were straight up and down, like walls. You had to pay attention riding [horseback] in that country." Tony sat quietly for a few moments. "Miles City country, there's nothing quite like it."

Eastern Montana is 100,000 square miles, larger than all but seven of the other forty-nine states; but mention eastern Montana to an old cowhand and his mind slips naturally to Miles City. Set among rolling hills just south of the Yellowstone River in the heart of southeastern Montana's big grass country, Miles City became well known in the 1880s and 1890s as the final destination for the great Texas–Montana trail drives. I've met at least a dozen old hands who traveled through or worked out of Miles City before World War I. They concur with Tony Grace that the Miles City area had the best grass, the most horses, the worst water (alkali) and that the roundup season had the earliest wake-up hours and the most rain. But there was more to it than that. More than one old hand told me that if you stay quiet enough long enough, the land in eastern Montana speaks back.

Rivers define the "Big Open," photographer L.A. Huffman's term for the land around his home base of Miles City. A careful look at a map of Montana shows the Big Open as a huge piece of land shaped like an arrowhead—the point of the arrowhead sitting just east of the Montana border, where the

Yellowstone joins the Missouri; the northern border is defined by the Missouri, south is the Yellowstone with the Musselshell to the west.

Rivers often define Montana's spaces. Old hands mention their names with familiarity, just as with favorite horses or old Stetsons. Joe Hughes worked the Bighorn, Tony Grace and Art Wahl the Tongue and Powder rivers. Those three rivers, flowing north into the mighty Yellowstone, figure prominently in cowboy songs, poems and stories. The Milk River flowed south into the Missouri up along the "hi-line," where Mary Welte lived as a cowhand's wife (see pages 83 and following). The Marias, Teton, Sun and Smith rivers run east into the Missouri near Great Falls, defining the country most oldtimers think of as Charlie Russell's. The Judith, along with the Musselshell, define fertile central Montana, where Tony Grace first landed at Roundup when he came west in 1907.

It wasn't uncommon for old hands to leave the plains and settle on smaller spreads in mountainous western Montana. Winters there are milder. Still, many would second the sentiment of "Wild Horse" Wes Wright that being on that western side of the Rockies is "jes' like being in a big corral."

The cowboy was my hero when I was just a kid.
To me, romance and glamour shown on everything he
did...

—J.K. Ralston

Kenny Trowbridge saved this photograph of XIT roundup wagons
and 165 saddle horses between Culbertson and Poplar in 1900.
His collection was donated to the Hamilton County Museum,
Ravalli, and the image is reproduced with their permission.

Introduction

Those first two lines from a short poem by Cowboy Hall of Fame artist J.K. Ralston hold true for a lot of Americans. As kids, many of us dreamed about becoming horseback cowboys on the western plains. J.K. came from a time when it was still possible. Grandson of Montana pioneers, he grew up on horses in the early 1900s and was a real cattle-roping cowboy by age fourteen.

Everything in this book is taken from old cowhands like J.K. They lived it, and they told it straight. There are two ways of talking for old hands—outright lies ("big windies") and unvarnished truth. They told me both.

Much of the information came from Tony Grace, born in 1890 into a Polish-immigrant city family. He decided he wanted to be a cowboy at age nine. Good-natured and inquisitive, young Tony had seen posters around Milwaukee that captured his imagination. They pic-

tured a man standing tall in woolly chaps, boots and a starched felt high-brimmed hat. Tony always could see that picture in his mind. The exact wording escaped him, but it was something like "Nature created a man like this and called him a cowboy."

It was 1899, movies weren't promoting the cowboy myth yet, but the poster was enough. Tony wanted to be a man like that—nature's creation, a hard-working, horse-loving warrior of the plains. His only riding experience had been on a merry-go-round, but Tony worked his way west on the railroad at seventeen, landed a ranch-hand job in Roundup, in central Montana, and learned to rope and ride.

Tony wasn't expecting glamour. He wanted to work with horses and cattle, and that was what he got. That first season he developed what he called his "affinity to the horse and allergy to the pitchfork." From then on, he worked as a cowhand. Cowhands don't pitch hay, unless it can be done from horseback. They herd cattle. Tony called them cow chaperones. During his seventy-year cattle career, Tony worked in six western states, retiring in his late eighties with his wife Viola to the small logging town of Darby in the mountains of southwestern Montana. Tony always planned to live to 100, a mile mark he easily achieved. He attributed his long life and good health to taking things as they came—and drinking a cup of hot water each morning, a habit he picked up in his twenties from an older hand nicknamed Hot Water Howard.

If any disproved the myth of the bumbling cowboy, it was Tony. He was articulate and smart. His insights came from a lifetime of working outside with horses and cattle. He worked with people, too. He married and took up wrangling cattle and dudes after retiring at around age 40 from a cowhand's single life. He told me people are like horses: all different, but all wondering what's going on and responding to the right treatment.

Old hands lament the loss of common sense in contemporary society. Tony claimed there's too much school and too little learning these days. Buckaroos of Tony's time lived close to the land. In that way, they resembled Indians (which many of them were) more than they did Hollywood's cowboys.

"The worst thing that happened to the cowboy was the dime novel, then Hollywood got in the act," Tony said. Fixing the beam of his blue eyes on me, he delighted in setting the cowboy record straight.

The record could use some straightening. Retired cowboys tend to take it easy, and seldom grumble about things they can't do anything about. But, like Tony, they resent the huge gap between cowboy myth and actuality. J.K. Ralston was the most outspoken on that topic. He snorted about the "sad stuff circulated about cowboys" and was apt to get upset by the very word: "We never called ourselves that! We were filly chasers, ranahans, cowhands, waddies, buckaroos, bronc peelers..."

J.K. claimed that few who didn't live it understand what the life was like, writers least of all. When he saw that I was willing to listen, he was more than willing to talk.

Where do I come in? Born in Iowa, raised in Wisconsin, I moved west to finish college in the early 1960s, and stayed. It was the name that brought me—with a name like Montana, it had to be the last frontier. Although I spent twelve years on a ranch and love the life, I'm more interested in ten-speeds than horses. I didn't choose the cowboy subject, it chose me.

Let me tell you about Joe Hughes, because he started it all, sitting on a park bench in my adopted hometown of Hamilton, Montana, eating strawberries and ice cream with his wife, Pearl. They were quite a picture—Joe in new Levi's, suit jacket and old-style black felt cowboy hat with a "pencil curl" brim, Pearl in a pretty print dress and tiny veiled hat.

I had asked to take their photograph that day in the park, and Joe grinned. "Sure, if you're not worried about breaking your Kodak." A crafts fair was going on, and Joe had been demonstrating the art of knotting and braiding rawhide and rope. Old hands are all good at it. Joe was a master.

That was in the mid-1960s. The old couple still lived on the ranch where Joe had grown up, the place where he wrote his first poem at age seven, tied his baby sister Mary's sled to a cow's tail, and learned his four older brothers' motto, "Careful what ya rope, ya gotta ride it."

Over the years, Joe told me stories about early cowhands, never quite figuring out why I was interested. "We were nuthin' special, honey, just the hardest-workin' and the lowest-paid men on the job scale."

Nuthin' special? I knew better. I followed Joe from his ranch to the tiny bungalow he and Pearl later rented in town and—after Pearl died—to the silver trailer parked in a backyard carport, and finally to a hospital room where Joe had an oxygen tank parked next to his bed. Joe recalled old poems he'd learned in cow camps—"They tell it best," he'd say as he served me tea with cream in his one china cup, or wine and whatever simmered on the stove (usually a good stew he called mulligan).

Meeting Joe and other old-time cowhands presented me with a chicken-egg proposition: Did cowboying make good men or did good men become cowboys? Joe scoffed at my notion that cowboys in the early 1900s were all good men. He told me that his brother Frank was the best bronc peeler and meanest man he ever met. I told him the mean ones all must have died off young.

Joe died in 1984 at age ninety-one. If cowboys survived their early heydays, they seemed to live forever. The old hands of my acquaintance mostly lived into their nineties. They worked cows in the chuck wagon style, a method that generally bit the dust in the early 1920s with changes brought about by mechanization following World War I, but a method still found in remote pockets of the West.

Many of the buckaroos whose stories are in this book lived within a few hours drive of my home. It's cowboy heaven. Big-scale ranching may have taken place on the plains of eastern Montana, but old hands went out to pasture in the forested western mountains.

When I decided to tell the cowboys' own story, one thing bothered me. How could I set the record straight with firsthand accounts when there weren't supposed to be any "real" cowboys after 1889, or at the latest, 1900? Historians of the northern plains killed off the cowboy era with the cattle-killing "Hard Winter of 1886-1887," when so many cattle companies went under, or with the arrival of fences and homesteaders beginning a decade later.

As usual with a question of historical significance, I went to my friend and mentor K. Ross Toole.

Ross was the feisty grandson of Montana Irish pioneers, a gifted scholar and conservationist known for his articulate fervor and knowledge concerning the West. His western history classes at the University of Montana often were jammed with a thousand students, phenomenal for a student body of 6,000, and his books on the West found national audiences. I visited Ross and his wife, Joan, at their Flathead Lake home in July 1982. Joan said it was his "last good talk." He went into the hospital the following day and gave up his battle against cancer a month later. He was 59.

I asked Ross why historians pulled such an early curtain on the cowboy era.

"It's the academic approach," he explained. "Statistically it's all right, but it's way off mark in reality because it doesn't take people into account. It overlooks that there is a real continuity from the 1890s into the 1910s and '20s. Ranchers might have gone from twelve thousand to twelve hundred head after that tough winter, but they survived. Unfortunately, TV and pulp western fiction are also based on an open-range era that is incredibly short, only about twelve years or so. In reality, the cowboy survived..."

"I'm too sentimental about that surviving cowboy." I said it like a confession. My desire was to write an objective book.

"Don't try to change that feeling," he replied. He said too many modern writers were attempting to redefine the American cowboy as a quick-tempered little bully or a buffoon.

Ross knew cowboys firsthand. He grew up on a ranch, a life that he and Joan later shared. "The old hands I knew as a kid are among the finest men I've ever known," Ross said. "They shouldn't be debunked. Cowboys were men in search of freedom. They rode beautifully, worked mind-boggingly; their lives could be extraordinarily dangerous. Their word meant something. There's a closer connection between the romantic-man-on-horseback cowboy myth and cowboy actuality than any other myth I can think of."

Trouble is, Hollywood myth makers and pulp writers ignored the real cowboy, who would have made an excellent hero, and they created a gunslinging villain. This book presents the cowboy's own story as told by the old-timers, the last horseback cowboys. The reader can create myths and heroes from there.

It was the freedom that got to a guy.

—Tony Grace

Donovan McGee, aged 18 months in 1909, considers the mule. Courtesy of Donovan McGee

How Boys Became Cowboys

The year was 1907. Art Wahl was tired of milking cows. Fifteen seemed the right age to go alone to America and become a real cowboy. His parents didn't say much; after all, an older brother had left home as a teenager. And Norwegians figure if things haven't taken by that age, they never will. There was a "goodbye, son" and passage to the new country.

No one asked Art how a Norwegian kid knew about cowboying, not until I showed up at his roominghouse in Missoula, Montana in 1980. He peered at me through thick glasses for what seemed like several minutes. Finally he smiled and said with his slight accent, "I knew all about it through those books."

"The dime novels?" I persisted, wondering if at least that part of the cowboy legend was true. Did young men actually read sensational accounts of cowboy life and head west?

"Ya. I came over to become a cowboy and kill Indians."

Trouble was, Art first went to the wrong part of the country. Wisconsin was where all the Norwegians on the ship were headed, so he went there. He found milk cows and teams of tired, stolid work horses, just like home. But he quickly learned that the cowboys and Indians were all out west, and he patiently milked cows and saved pennies for two years to make enough money to travel to Montana by train.

Miles City was his destination, a regular watering hole for working cowhands. I asked how he came to choose it.

He shrugged. "Heard of it on the way out."

A job for a cowhand in the plains around Miles City was a sure thing during spring and fall roundups. If a buckaroo came to town and couldn't find work herding cattle, chances were he could break horses. Art had chosen the high plains' horse-selling center, where 3,000 head were purchased monthly by buyers from places like St. Louis, Paris and London.

A cowboy himself didn't buy horses (unless he was a greenhorn and didn't know any better) for two reasons. First of all, the last thing a cowhand needed was a horse. His own personal string came with the job. Big outfits had remudas of several hundred saddle horses trailing after their chuck wagons. Horses, like chickens and humans, have pecking orders and the rancher did not welcome strange animals upsetting the balance. The second reason not to own a horse was financial. Horses went cheap in Montana in the early 1900s, at five or ten dollars a head, but if a hand owned one (called a "private"), it was up to him to board it out while he was trailing cattle, hard to do on a wage of twenty to forty bucks a month.

A cowboy without a horse? Joe Hughes first told me that fact and he never exaggerated. "We were too poor to have our own horses," he scoffed, and I didn't want to believe him. It took a while to let go of that part of the myth.

Cowboys loved horses, and they always ended up owning some of their own. But not while they worked roundups. Working hands were young, single and horseless. Horses (and wives) slowed a cowboy down between jobs. Herding cows was seasonal, with spring and fall roundups the busy times. Cowhands were mobile, trekking from job to job. Men who took to the saddle were gypsies, always ready for new country, usually traveling distances too great for a horse. Truth is, they traveled by train, just as Art did. As early as 1880 and the great trail drives, hands trailed cattle north and bought train tickets back south (unless they chose to brave Montana's alkaline water and cold winters, both reputed to take the meanness out of a guy).

Hollywood gave us plenty of train scenes. We saw cowboy-villains rob trains and cowboy-heroes capture train robbers and rescue pretty ladies from train tracks. But I don't recall seeing a cowboy board a train, throw his saddle in a vacant seat, stretch, yawn, sit down and fall asleep.

"Were they shootin' it up in Miles City when you got off the train?" I asked Art.

"Nope."

"Things were pretty quiet, pretty tame?"

"Ya."

"What about the Indians you were looking for?"

"They were all herded off to reservations."

Art said "day" for "they" and "vere" for "were." He was of so few words that a single episode from his life took a day to relate—not a day of work, but a day of hanging out: late-morning chat with Art, Velveeta cheese sandwiches and soup prepared by his elderly landlady, Jessie, after-lunch chat and coffee, a drive downtown where Art played poker daily in a bar. He had such extraordinary luck that no one would play him for high stakes. He used to make $350 every weekend, playing Friday until Monday morning. "I picked up a little over twenty thousand dollars," he told me.

"And you didn't cheat, either."

"Oh, no, I don't know how to cheat."

I asked Art if he was disappointed all those years ago when he discovered the reality of a cowhand's life. He shook his head.

"What'd you like about it?"

A few moments of thought, a gentle reply, "I just liked it."

We sat in the comfort of overstuffed chairs, quietly watching the tape recorder go around. I wondered if Art were back on the trail, squatting by the fire. (Cowboys didn't sit, they squatted. I think it kept them limber, or at least able to walk.)

Art broke the silence, "It was the freedom, that and working with horses and cattle and good men."

"Did you ever see any gunplay?"

Art shook his head.

A cowhand might own a gun, but it was too heavy and cumbersome for the trail. He wore it for photographs or during signpost-shooting trips to town. It was fun to shoot out signs, but hands preferred ropes over guns. Roping required a cowboy's skill, and it was safer. Joe Hughes shot a pipe out of his ornery older brother's mouth while playing with a rusty six-shooter at age seven. "That," he said, "ended my gunfighting career."

Old hands scoff at the notion of cowboy as gunfighter. Joe said he nev-

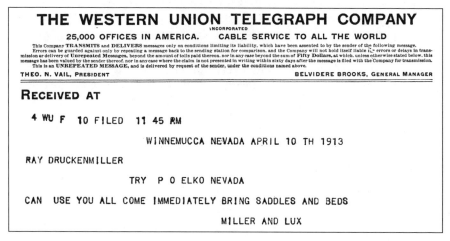

Tony Grace preserved this telegram that brought work for him and other hands in the spring of 1913.

er laid eyes on a man with two six-shooters, that a gun on each hip was strictly a Hollywood invention, and if a cowboy did wear guns that way it's because a movie star did it first.

Art arrived in Miles City in May, the best time for spring roundup work. A livery stable owner gave young Art a stall to sleep in and assured him there were lots of riding jobs. When a trail boss rode into town on a two-horse wagon the next day, looking for a cowhand, Art didn't tell him the only horses he ever had sat were tired old work horses.

"Didn't he ask if you could ride?"

Art grinned. "Nope."

Art didn't ask any questions either. He had all a cowhand needed when he rolled out of town on a wagon loaded with supplies the next morning—a saddle, a bedroll and a job. He didn't ask his new boss which outfit he was working for or where they were headed. It's easy to imagine the two men exchanging nothing but "yup" and "nope" during their two-day drive.

When they arrived at a lonesome spot on the prairie, Art assumed the chuck wagon that fed him and nine other men three square meals a day was the only chuck wagon. Imagine his (poker-faced) surprise to see twenty-one more wagons at the fall rendezvous six months later. "And they were eight or nine men to a wagon, so you can see how big the outfit was. I found out I was working for the C-K outfit, biggest spread in Montana. They had forty thousand head, and that was after a sixty percent loss from a hard winter," Art said in what was possibly his longest monologue to me.

Art started out as a wrangler, a new-boy position that involved moving and pasturing the horses. By the time the rendezvous rolled around, Art might not have been a full-fledged cowboy, but he was established as a top bronc rider. Contrary to the notion of the cowboy on a bucking bronco, many hands preferred a buckless horse. Cattle are easily frightened, and well-broken horses are best on the job. Every hand at one time or another had to deal with a bucking horse, but they didn't all like it. Breaking horses takes a certain skill. Art had it.

"How'd you do it?"

Art was quiet for a few minutes. "I guess I could set a horse."

"Did you have to get rough, show the horse who's boss?"

"Nope."

"You were always gentle?"

"Ya."

"Did you talk to the horse?"

"Ya. All the time."

"In English or Norwegian?"

"Norwegian."

Art was the youngster of the crew, so I asked how the older hands regarded his innate horse sense. "When we had a real buckin' horse and some fella would get on him, the other men would say, 'Aw, you can't ride him, let Swede do it'." Art looked at me, the idea of a Norwegian being called "Swede" still giving him an incredulous look. "That's what they called me. 'Swede'."

Cowhands all had nicknames. Buck, Slim, Tex. New boys were often called Kid, Button or Pistol. Swede was a compliment, even though a Norwegian could take it otherwise. New boys often were kidded, the butts of practical jokes, although I doubt if Art was. No one ever recalls seeing him angry, but even his silences convey the impression that no one ever pushed him around.

Cowherding was a singular way of life. Men either got out early and took up marriage and ranching, like Joe, or stayed and married late, like Tony Grace and Art. Both of them were forty when they settled down to ranches and families, and both married younger women. Art's wife was from his hometown in Norway, but he met her in the States.

"Did you know her at home?" I asked.

He fixed me with that quizzical, intelligent look of his and smiled, "Ach, she wasn't even born yet when I left."

Still, he outlived her. Art emerged almost untouched from a lifetime of breaking rough horses—he even rode his favorite horse into a Missoula bar (no problem, since he owned the bar)—but shortly after his lively, much-loved wife Borghild ("Bert") died in 1976, he was run over by a pickup truck and suffered a punctured kidney, three broken ribs, multiple leg fractures, and a broken shoulder. "The only thing that hurt was the shoulder," he insisted. Doctors sent him to a nursing home, figuring healing would take two months minimum. In two weeks and two days, Art was out and walking upstairs to his boardinghouse room.

For every boy like Art and Tony who chose the cowboy life, a boy like J.K. Ralston or Joe was born to it. "Nuthin' else to do," Joe said. J.K. was riding with a roundup association called the Pot Hounds at age twelve, on his home territory along the Missouri River in northeastern Montana. His recollection about the new-boy feeling of finding a job with a big outfit filled in the gaps left by Art's yups and nopes.

"Say you and me are boys from Nebraska, what we wanna do is punch cows. We got a bedroll and a saddle. Go to the livery stable, they tolerate us, might let us roll our bed down. First thing we do is go into a bar and realize the bartender is an old cowpuncher. 'You fellows lookin' for a job?' 'Yuh, we want a job.' 'Well, '79 wagon be in one of these days, maybe LU-Bar wagon.' We're in the bar later and the bartender says, 'There comes the boss right now,' and he introduces us to the boss. Boss buys us a drink and we stand there a little bit. Finally, okay, he takes us on. Says, 'Tomorrow the mess wagon will be in here to outfit, when it comes you can get with the cook, put your stuff in the wagon and ride out with him'."

The new boys arrived at a spot on the prairie, fifty miles from town. J.K. described the crew of nine or ten men as a "mixed bag." "It wasn't a proposition like any other business where people been working for you five or ten years. There might be three or four new fellas like you and me, maybe a guy who's rode for 'em before and he's perfectly comfortable. Fellas who work for the outfit year-round are still in town, maybe still on a drunk or visitin' the girls. Most of them already have their strings but you and I haven't got anything."

Uppermost on a hand's mind were the horses that would be divvied out. Would he be able to handle his first horse? Would he pull leather (grab the saddle horn) or, worse yet, get bucked through camp? A cowhand's personal string ranged from three to five horses in the southwest United States or nine to eleven in Montana, where grazing land was vast. The morning of the first roundup, the boss gave each man a circle horse. If a hand knew what to do, he put his rope under the boss's rope and over the horse's head so the boss could go on to the next man. If he didn't know what to do, he watched, and probably muttered a few prayers.

"Us new birds," J.K. said, "we're gonna get some rough ones, don't think we aren't. The two or three old hands, you might call 'em pensioners, they get the best ones, darn right they do. You and me are gonna get these spoiled horses and when he leads one out, if the boss was like old Matt Rogue, he says to you, 'This horse is gentle.' Once in a while he might be, but it was damn seldom."

Eastern Montana was famous for good chuck wagon cooking and early hours. The day started as early as three o'clock in the morning. "That first morning you look that first horse all over because you're gonna hafta catch him and it'll be about four days later and you're gonna hafta pick him outa a hundred-sixty or -seventy head o' horses in that corral and it isn't going to be quite daylight."

The chuck wagon moved twice a day during a full-scale roundup and with each move the new hand got another horse. "You keep drawin' and drawin' 'til you've got your full string. If you get a full string of eleven horses you'll get four cow horses, five circle horses and two night horses," J.K. explained.

A man's string was his "property" as long as he worked for an outfit. Rustling was not uncommon, but not even the boss borrowed from a hand's string without permission.

All this sounds complicated on paper, but J.K. said it went off like clockwork. "It's like nothing you'll ever do again, you find out with a well-run cow outfit what a pleasure it is to work for 'em. Poorly-run outfits? They went outa business."

Boys like Tony, who had never been around horses but became cowboys, often developed immediate, uncanny rapport with horses. "Weren't you banking a lot on the fact you'd like horses? What if you hadn't liked them?" I asked Tony.

"There was no doubt in my mind, I knew I was gonna like 'em." Tony grinned, "I was a typical hand, I'd go to any extreme to stay on horseback."

Tony was born in 1890, Art in 1891. Unlike Art and most of the boys of their generation, Tony had a realistic idea of a working cowhand's job. Tony was well-read, and as a young teen dismissed dime novels as "so much hooey" but read everything else about the West he could find in Milwaukee. An article in a weekly tabloid, the *Police Gazette,* portraying the life of a working hand from Cody, Wyoming, was enough to set the record straight for young Tony.

"I wasn't expecting the romantic part at all. Riding a horse, working on a horse, that's what appealed to me."

Tony was built like a typical hand—of small stature with the almost-dainty feet a cowboy took pride in. Tony at ninety-seven patted his belly and said it was the only thing that changed since steer-wrestling days. Tony had lived in the West all but seventeen of his years but still approached the life of a cowboy with new-boy curiosity. His eyes were wide open, his mind sharp, memory phenomenal.

Tony's first season in the West was as a ranch hand. He described the job—"If there's hay to pitch, you pitch it, sheep to tend, you tend 'em. The ranch owner gave me a horse to ride and, believe me, I was in the saddle whenever possible."

Modern cowboys are all ranch hands, doing whatever needs to be done. In Tony's day, it was possible to be a cowhand and just work cows, at least from spring through fall roundups. After one season as a ranch hand, Tony graduated to big outfits and during his long career worked as herder, wrangler, bronc buster (although he said he never *broke* horses, he "gentled" them) and finally, chuck wagon cook. But he didn't pitch hay again until he retired at around age forty to his own ranch.

Tony said it was almost impossible to ask a cowhand to turn in his boots

Montana-born Joe Hughes was 17 and an eastern Montana cowhand when he posed for this portrait in 1910. Author's collection

for a desk job. He summed up the attraction of cowherding and why so many hands "retired" to ranching:

"It was the freedom that got to a guy. As a cowboy, you were your own boss, sent off by yourself to ride the range. You knew what you had to do but you made your own decisions. Didn't work by the clock, got up at a certain time but went on from there, quit when you were finished. Near Miles City where the day began at three a.m. you were often done around three in the afternoon. Having your own ranch you worked 'round the clock some seasons, but you were still your own boss, you still worked outside and you were on horseback much of the time."

Nowadays, a guy'd lie on credit if he got cash for tellin' the truth.

Joe Hughes

The poker game is off to a dangerous start in this gag photo taken in a Jackson Hole bunkhouse one Christmastide. Tony Grace is the cowhand on the right, his pal Dewey Van Winkle on the left. Courtesy of Tony Grace

The Code

Cowhands started off young, but perhaps they didn't all start off honorable. A strong code of cow camp ethics nudged them in the right direction. It's not easy to pin down this cowboy code. Rules weren't always written out and stuck to the canvas wall of the chuck wagon, but were passed along by example. The older men defined the code by their actions.

"My way was always to look up to the old hands, and I never had any reason to be sorry," cowboy-artist J.K. Ralston said.

While on the trail after the code, I asked old-timers what traits cowhands had in common. Tony Grace said cussing, Joe Hughes advised me to forget about cowboys ("We lacked brains; if I'd any more sense I woulda been a half-wit") and Art Wahl didn't say anything. J.K. warned me to not lump cowhands together, "Nobody gets the cowboy right, especially writers. We were all different human beings like you and me."

J.K. had my attention, and he wasn't finished. This was back in the days when he didn't quite trust me. Later, he would tell me his secrets, but that day he looked down his imperious beak at me and I understood why fellow hands tagged him Curlew ("I had a long beak and I was singin' all the time."). J.K., the noble old bird, said sadly, "The cowboy, he's been told in lots and lots of ways. In truth, he was a different proposition altogether."

J.K. knew I was working on a "cowboy project." I didn't tell him my intention was to set the record straight. It seemed wise not to talk about it.

Setting things straight meant unraveling the code. I never doubted the existence of such a code, not because the myth says so but because old cowhands have more in common than low-riding Levi's and a straight-backed bend from the hips.

For example, their easy-going, take-it-in-stride attitude. "Were we easy-goin' as young hands? Generally, yes," Tony said. "Just like anyplace else, you'd see all kinds—hot tempers, mild tempers—but about the only thing you worried about was the next horse, whether you could set him or not."

Old hands talk straight (unless an outrageous tall tale is in the telling), laugh easily, see humor in everyday occurrences, keep both their word and their cool, and display decency towards women, children and horses. All these traits, plus similarities in stories and reminiscences, spell out one thing—cowhand society allowed total freedom as long as members respected a few rules.

The code was based on trust. It was tough enough dealing with Ma Nature, touchy cows and motherless calves without wondering if your partner or his word could be trusted.

As Tony put it, "Straightforward and honest? Very much so, more so than the general run of men in that day. However, that applied not only to the cowpunchers but to other old-timers living in the country. I've seen a million dollars worth of cattle sold on a man's word."

Joe Hughes had so little time for liars that he even expressed annoyance at his sister's embellishment of tales from their rough-and-ready childhood. "I'd just like to be remembered as a square shooter. I figure honesty and integrity is a good thing for any man to say he had. Nowadays, a guy'd lie on credit if he got cash for tellin' the truth. My mother taught me that a liar is worse than a thief."

Honesty simplifies life. A deal was confirmed with a handshake (Kenny Trowbridge bought his bungalow that way when he settled in Darby in the

1940s). A foreman could dump wages in a sack on the ground, and the men would help themselves as they rode into camp (perhaps small wages help keep men honest). Tony joined hundreds of cowhands—including Art Wahl, although they did not meet there—at Camp Lewis in Washington in 1917 to train horses for World War I cavalry forces. The hands quickly turned to poker as a pastime, just as they did in the bunkhouses back home. "The chips and the money used by the dealer was put in a cigar box and set on a window sill," Tony explained. "Nobody ever thought of taking any...'til they started sending men in from the cities—that changed the picture fast. We started losing things. The money had to be locked away. I lost a bridle that I had to pay for."

In cow camp, a man's name or background never was asked. Judging a man by his face is an old habit and, as Joe said, "A fella's actions tell all you ever need to know." Cowhands often came from less than lily-white backgrounds. Many ran away from mean fathers or stepfathers or from the law. The first time I interviewed Joe, he teased, "Better not use my name, there might be some old-time sheriffs still around."

As a kid, Joe knew some tough characters who worked seasonally on the ranch, usually Irishmen and always hired out of his father's favorite saloon. "There was this pirate...his ears were pulled way out from wearin' rings in 'em, he used to talk about sailing ships, worked on slave ships. I don't know if you could come right out and say he was a pirate, you more or less figured he was. He told about fightin', capturin' a ship, sang all the old sailing songs."

Another of the seasonal hands was a gunfighter. "He had two holes through him, both from forty-five's, didn't leave much of a hole goin' in but sure left a mean-lookin' scar coming out. He was quiet, I'd work on him to tell me stories...he'd talk about the Rock, he spent time in the territorial prison in Yuma, Arizona. Imagine how hot that would be in the summertime, no air conditioning," Joe laughed. "He warned me to stay outa trouble, I was just a kid and I got him to talk more'n anybody. Like him? Darn right I liked him, he was a good guy and a top hand, could set any horse. I waited for him to come back, he was usually sporting more bullet holes."

In more than ninety years, Joe met only that one gunfighting cowhand. And that fellow didn't wear a gun, at least not near the ranch.

Tony had expected to see more gun play in the West. "I've seen very few guns from here to Arizona. In six western states I don't believe I've seen more than a dozen men carrying a gun. Some owned 'em all right, but the gun was either in the bunkhouse at the ranch or it was in his war bag in[side] his bedroll."

But Tony recalled a happy-ending shooting that took place in Nevada.

"A fella in a mining camp had a reputation of being a gunman. Had everybody in town pretty well shy of him, he was quick going for that gun. He threatened his wife one too many times and she got a gun and killed him. When they started for the cemetery with the body, they stopped for several rounds of drinks at the saloon. When they were lowering him in the hole, they were singing 'Turkey in the Straw.' His wife? No, she wasn't charged with anything. She was a heroine."

I'd been wanting to talk to an old-time law officer about gunslinging cowboys but had about given up when I met Donovan McGee in Juneau, Alaska.

Don's three-year career as a deputy sheriff began in 1927 when he was only nineteen. Wyoming-born, wild-Irish Don was breaking spoiled horses for rancher John Biggs outside of Burns, a raw eastern Oregon cowtown Don described as "right out of 1890," when he saw Sheriff Charlie Frazier approaching.

Back home, Don had run with a pack of wild hooligans who managed to stay in trouble and sometimes landed in jail. He said only dumb luck kept Don himself from behind bars. So he wondered "Uh-oh, what have I been up to?" To his surprise, the sheriff offered him a job.

"I need a deputy and a jailer, you know all the boys..." the sheriff said. And he offered Don $125 a month, big money in those days. Don said he thought "fine and dandy," but told Sheriff Frazier he'd have to talk to his boss first.

Boss Biggs said, "It's a good job, take it."

Don's buddies did not seem to resent his job as deputy. He recalled being handcuffed to one of them, a fellow named Trout who was caught running horses and was being transported to the penitentiary. The road was little more than a cowpath, and the young deputy and the young horse thief bumped along in the back seat of the sheriff's car.

Don recalled, "I said, 'How's it going, Trout?' He was good-natured, always singing and making up songs. I'll never forget the one he came out with, he made it up as we were rolling along. To have that kind of spirit in his situation..."

And sixty years later Don sang me Trout's song in a rich Irish tenor.

> *Farewell, lovely ladies, farewell.*
> *Goodbye, I shall see thee no more.*
> *Goodbye to each blond and brunette,*
> *Goodbye to each chippie and whore.*

You who are possessed of a treasure,
Possessor of which I would be,
And I'll show you the way to true pleasure,
If you step in the backroom with me.

I asked Don if gunslinging played a part in a cowtown. "No, that notion is highly overrated. Cowboys tended to settle things among themselves. Except in Texas—they were still fighting the Civil War down there. They were raised with guns."

Don did recall one shooting match, he called it "the only thing Prineville, Oregon has for renown." In that central Oregon town, a sheepman got into an argument with a cowboy from the ZX spread south of Bend, Oregon (owned by Texans) and they decided to settle it with guns. They were facing each other across a table, and the agreement was that each man would grab one end of a handkerchief and shoot off his gun.

"Of course they couldn't miss, being that close. Still, one lived through it. Which one? The sheepman." Don shook his head and laughed, "Being from Texas and letting a sheepman kill you—he probably didn't go to heaven."

When asked about shootings, old hands often came up with love-triangle tragedies. Don's story in this vein had an unusual twist. "The old buckaroo boss for the TA [ranch] was having a love affair with the ranchhand's wife. The hand heard about it, shot both of them and himself." Nothing too unusual in that. But the twist offers further evidence that cowboys weren't gunmen—all three parties lived.

"I used to kid the guy about it, you could see the old forty-five slug in the back of his neck. He stayed on as foreman."

"What about the other two?"

"Oh, the husband insisted that they get married."

I figured that part of the code was beyond me.

Defending your honor with your fists was not the cowboy's style, either. Again, the movies have it all wrong. Fist fights among cowhands were almost as unusual as gunfights, perhaps because it's not possible to fight on horseback. The exceptions were the Irish hands of Joe's childhood, who fought all the time.

"Did you ever fight?" I asked Joe.

"No, I ran. My feet could never stand to see my face abused," he replied.

Don McGee was an Irishman who liked to fight. "You don't have to whip everybody, just whip one real good," Don said.

A tough old granddad took in Don, his mother and three siblings after

Don's father died. "He worked on the assumption, 'I'm the boss, that's it,' and wasn't above using a quirt to prove it," Don said. "There were seventeen or eighteen kids in a small school building, [and] six of us boys were giving the teacher a hard time. My sister was the stool pigeon...My grandfather got some neighbor men together. They rode up, tied their horses outside. 'Miss Schultz, we'd like to speak to some of your students.' He took a quirt to us. I can still hear his deep voice as he left, 'If you ever have any trouble, let us know'."

Young Donovan developed a sensitive nature with a black side to it. "My grandmother was full-blooded Iroquois. I'm a quarter, but there's no proof. Only one aunt was proud of it, the rest said we're French. My granddad came from Ireland. He married an Indian but 'squaw man' were fighting words to him. He raised a bunch of mean McGees."

"You're not mean."

"I got over it. When I was a little kid, I had a terrible temper. In grade school the teacher said to my mother, 'You must talk to Donovan, he cries when I talk about two babes in the woods who died and the robins covered them with leaves...and later in the day he'll bash some kid's head in'."

Boxing curbed Don's fighting instincts. He arrived in Burns on the Fourth of July, 1926. A celebration was going on in the rough and woolly town (the railroad had reached there only the year before) and when a fighter didn't show up for an outdoor boxing match, Don took up the challenge. He said his opponent was a skinny kid just out of the Navy, who used him for a punching bag. But Don boxed and he won, and the town made him a hero.

A cowhand's life was seasonal, allowing lots of time for other pursuits. Don worked cattle, broke horses and followed athletic shows. Outdoor boxing matches were as popular as rodeos. He sent his earnings home to his mother, two sisters and kid brother.

"I fought sheepherders, cowboys. It helped my terrible temper. In all, I fought close to fifty fights. I had a real good record."

Don never did get into a fight in a cow camp, and he said the few he knew about were a result of cabin fever. He recalled working with two other fellows who had been holed up together over New Year's in a bunkhouse and weren't speaking. When it came time to move the cattle, the man more or less in charge had to break the three-day silence. He told Don to go on swing and when he gave directions to the other cowhand, his partner in cabin fever, the man took offense and started punching.

Don laughed at the memory. "He was insulting him, 'You Indian S.O.B. You won't tell me what to do.' Funny thing, all three of us were part Indian. I stayed out of the way. It was sloppy, wet snow, they were rolling around in the slush. No way could they hurt each other. One got his nose bloodied. Fighting blew off all the steam and they got along fine after that."

Tony Grace had to give the matter some thought when asked about fist fights. He recalled a cow foreman, Joe Graham, who got into an argument over the Ku Klux Klan. "I suppose the other guy was a Texan, I know Joe wasn't. Anyway, they got into a fist fight. The next day Joe said, 'Ya know that was the best fight I was ever in. Every time I got up that bird knocked me down—I didn't hafta do anything, he did it all'."

Tony said tempers flared hotter in the Southwest. "Perhaps," he mused, "it was all that liquid fire they doctored their food with."

Texas chili or Montana sourdough, western meals were meant to be shared. Joe said his gracious Irish mother never turned a man away without a meal, whether he sported bullet holes or not. Hospitality was the heart of the code. "I'd heard about western hospitality, but I was still surprised," Tony recalled. Strangers were seldom turned away. Doors went unlocked.

"People didn't even have keys. If you were out riding the range and somebody was home, chances are they'd ask you in," Tony said. "And if there wasn't anybody home, you'd go in and help yourself. All that was expected of you was to replace the kindling and do the dishes, leave the place the way you found it. I've eaten a meal in a stranger's house more than once, and I got it myself. It was the custom of the country."

Cowboy poet D.J. O'Malley penned this verse and pinned it on the tent of an old cowhand turned sheepherder back in 1897:

> *You, stranger, who comes to my tent*
> *I hope you ride away content.*
> *Eat all you want, my only wishes*
> *Are, when you're through you'll wash the dishes.*

Settlement and all that goes with it changed the open door policy of the West. Tony remembered an old-timer who exclaimed, "Talk about the West gettin' civilized! Now we gotta lock our chicken coops, that's civilization?"

"Roads fouled hospitality up quick," Tony said. "Good cars and roads. That and the poverty of overworked homesteaders. Once the homesteaders, or honyockers as they called 'em, came in and couldn't make it on unproductive land, some of them resorted to a little stealing on the side."

Braggarts became the butts of practical jokes and were laughed out of camp, if they got that far. Tony recalled a story from his Miles City days of two greenhorns who were laughed clear out of town.

"A lot of horses were brought in and sold to the armies, the French, the English, the Italians. Miles City was the range horse capital of the world at that time. There were quite a few riders, I was one of 'em. We had days when there wasn't any action at the stockyard, we'd be hanging around, mostly at the Tom Jones Saloon. A fella came in, said there were two new boys in town, braggin' about getting big jobs, wearing big hats with the tops folded back and red bandanas tied around their necks...I was sent over as a representative to the bar they were seen going into, I was supposed to invite them over to the Tom Jones, but I couldn't even start up a conversation with the two monkeys so we picked another fella to see if he could encourage 'em. This was Pinky Gist, a bronc rider, mostly bareback who later turned out to be a rodeo clown."

Pinky succeeded. He took the two swaggering but innocent greenhorns back to the Tom Jones, where a gambler who ran the game room posed as boss of the outfit all the other boys worked for. "One of the boys came in and said there was trouble back at the ranch, old Rain In The Face was on the warpath, and the buffalo got in the alfalfa, and there'd be hell to pay out at the ranch. Those two new boys were hired to work, fight Indians and run buffalo and they swallowed it. I left before they were through with 'em but several days later I saw Bob Finley, who was there that morning, and he said, 'I saw those two fellas, they were bulldozing sagebrush outside a town.' That means they got a job with a grub and hoe cutting sagebrush."

Complaining was just as bad as bragging. The prevailing attitude seemed to be, "There's always something to complain about, why bother?" Grudges were considered bad medicine around camp; it was better to forget squabbles.

Thus, life in a cow camp

Chuck Hayes. Photo by Jo Rainbolt

was seldom grim. Kenny Trowbridge, cowboy-historian-who'd-been-there and nationally-recognized storyteller, claimed authentic accounts of early trail drives didn't tell the real picture. "Sure, they was eatin' dust," Kenny bawled in his usual hearty way, "and scared of stampedes and floods and the like, but you kin jest bet they'd come ridin' in plumb beat after the worst catastrophe and some joker would turn the whole thing around. Have 'em all laughin'." Kenny knew cow camps; he started tagging after his father, a chuck wagon cook, in Idaho at age fourteen.

Stingy was a bad word. A tight guy had a "one-way pocketbook." Spending could be carried to extremes, making it impossible for a hand to make a stake, but the cowboy was young and living day to day so a bankroll didn't seem to matter. Loans were repaid, or the debtor might have to reckon with a cowhand's tendency to take the law into his own hands.

Old-timers just shake their heads when asked about today's emphasis on money, and they figure living on credit is plain haywire. They paid cash while making forty bucks a month, and they pay cash now.

Modern prices astound old hands. I met bachelor-cowboy Chuck Hayes on a downtown bench in Billings in 1984. Chuck, born into a Wyoming pioneer family in 1900, had arrived in Billings fifty-five years earlier when ham and eggs were a quarter, a room $2.50 a week. "You know, a hat like mine costs fifty dollars now, I dunno what's wrong with people. I priced a straw hat, twenty-four dollars, and they used to be a dollar ninety-eight. I tried to get a room one night: ten dollars. I'll sleep out before I give ten dollars for a room, I got a bedroll. A fella has to have five or six hundred dollars a month to live on."

I told him that's what writers and cowboys get along on, but other Americans figure they need three times that much.

A cowhand caught cheating at poker was in big trouble. In a hilarious reverse situation, Norwegian Art carefully retrieved money from the pocket of a sheriff's mackinaw after the pompous sheriff confiscated the hands' wages during a small-stakes poker game in Idaho. After redistributing their money to the crew, Art fled to Montana with the sheriff following him to the state line.

Rustling isn't an easy topic to work into a code of ethics. Kenny said that in his Idaho, small-scale rustling was tolerated, that a lot of early ranchers got started using a "long rope" on maverick (unbranded) cows and horses. He said a cowboy might pick up that "long rope" while out riding, and find a horse on the end of it when he got home. If the horse was a stray, the cowboy could keep it and his neck. If an owner appeared, the horse was returned.

Then there's the notion of the hard-drinking cowboy. It's not easy to erase the picture of a weary cowhand taking a nip from a flask, but (except for a medicinal bottle guarded by the cook) booze was not allowed in camp. Of course, dry camps made trips to town all the more appealing.

The code seemed to require men to sow wild oats during infrequent cattle-shipping trips to town. Everything you've seen in the movies about these trips is true. The town was painted red—signs and lamps shot out, saloons and girlie houses invaded. The foreman would make restitution for damages the following day. "We were young, healthy, in our prime and feelin' good about it…the sound of a harmonica could set us off," Tony explained.

Cowhands seldom stayed with one outfit very long, because there was too much country to see. But they were loyal to whatever outfit they worked for, a man would quit before he'd bad-mouth his outfit. Even Joe had to admit to this loyalty, the one attribute of the myth that he'd credit a real cowboy with: "I dunno where it sprung from but they were loyal, never put down their outfits." Money was obviously not a motivating factor. Tony said it was simple, a man wanted his outfit to look good, and as long as he worked for it he did his best to enhance the outfit's reputation.

Competition among outfits was keen. I've come across penciled versions of well-known trail songs where the C-K's, the LU Bars or 79's were extolled as "the best." A man's actions reflected on the whole outfit (apparently the crazier the action was in town, the more points). Tony said if a hand swore in front of a woman, another hand would call him on it. Kenny used "goddamn" as an adjective when he was a kid of seventy-five, but the older hands like Joe and Tony never cussed when I was around. J.K. said that when he was young, men couldn't even mention a T-shirt in front of a female.

"'Course some women could really cuss," Kenny bawled. "Now there was this Hickey Jones, fer Crischeezus she could outcuss any man."

Being a woman collecting stories about a man's culture seldom seemed a disadvantage. Joe Hughes sometimes balked when the bawdiness of a male society came up, but in general these old cowhands approached any topic head on. J.K. Ralston broached the most delicate subject during our first visit, when my colleague Michael Korn was out of the room. "Did you know…" he fixed his bushy-browed gaze on me, "that there were whorehouses in the cowtowns?" I hesitated a moment, then replied, "Yes, it's pretty common knowledge." J.K. leaned back in his chair and sighed, "That's a relief." What he meant, and later talked about, was his frustration towards an earlier double standard of women like his mother who, in his words, looked right through the prostitutes of Culbertson, pretending they weren't there.

Joe hesitated to sing dirty versions of trail songs when I was collecting songs with Korn, until I went out into the kitchen to help Kenny's wife Verna. An oft-repeated story features a hand who was fired for running out on a prostitute. The crew took up a collection and paid her.

"Women? Cowboys respected them. We washed our white shirts and got all spiffed up, got a haircut. I never did see a working cowboy with long hair. Cowboys had no trouble getting dances, no trouble finding ladies, if they were there," Tony said.

"The lone woman living out in the country never had to worry. Like schoolmarms, they seldom got lonely because there were so many bachelors. They got horses, saddles provided by the men."

When asked if cowboys were shy around women, Tony answered "no" at the same moment his wife Viola said "yes."

Cowboys are romantic; they like women. I think it started with their mothers. O'Malley's well-known poem "When the Work's All Done This Fall," a tear-jerker Joe approved of, features the sad fate of a hand who planned to go home to see his mother after the roundup. A rodeo steer-wrestler with nineteen-inch biceps got tears in his eyes when he told me how his ninety-year-old mother sang "Amazing Grace." Except for Paul Young, who must have set a record with his two marriages (thirty-two years in one, twenty-five in another, and stayed friends with both), the old hands I knew married for life. Joe said the thing he was proudest of was living with the best woman in the world, Pearl, for more than sixty years.

Donovan McGee married wrong the first time (a girl named Goldie). He met Alaska-born Rose in Juneau while on his way to South America after World War II and credited both his happiness and his geographic location to her. Don enjoyed a woman's company, as do all old hands. He said, "One change I appreciate is relaxing with women."

J.K. was happy with his life-mate, Willo, but he expressed envy over the freedom of today's youth and thought it was a good thing to be able to start over when things didn't work out.

Personal freedom brings to mind another rule of the code—"Don't mind anybody's business but your own." If two men did get into a fight, it was allowed to run its course unless a life was in danger. Under any circumstances, it was best not to offer help unless asked. Kenny said he learned that firsthand as a kid after offering to help an old hand who was mending his horse's headstall. "Son, if I'll be needin' your help I'll be askin' fer it," was the reply.

Just as etiquette dictated that a man's string of horses was his own and not to be used without permission, this held true for all a cowboy's few possessions: his horse tack—especially the saddle—his hat and bedroll.

But there was another side to these tough silent men who braved incredible temperatures, low pay, long hours and bizarre horse-related accidents, who rode alongside a partner all day without a word exchanged—these men were pranksters at heart. Age does not put out the devilish gleam in a cowhand's eye.

A cowhand's wit often caught up with him. He had an outlandish reputation to live up to—a result of the lies he made up about himself. Innocent bystanders often were taken in by richly-detailed stories about shootings, drinking bouts and train robberies. In a way, the cowboy created his own myth.

There were two modes of expression for the cowhand—simple truth or outright whopper. Honesty was the backbone of the code, humor the marrow.

Donovan McGee in 1988.
Photo by Jo Rainbolt

Without the horse, there wouldn't have been either cowboy or code. The way a man treated the animal that justified his existence said a lot about the man. Tony observed that hands careless toward horses and tack proved to be generally irresponsible. An insensitive rider could ruin a good horse, as could a show-off. The other hands often educated such types by getting them aboard the meanest, most wild-eyed broncs. Horses depended on men, so a good cowhand always put his horse's comfort before his own. Hands worked seven days a week on trail, no Sundays off, but horses got days off called "saddle breaks."

A motto of the code was "Not a horse that can't be rode, not a man that can't be throwed." And, of course, there was the unwritten rule every cowboy easily abided by: Never walk when you can ride. The horse gave a man stature; a horse was good company, easy to talk to and inclined to understand. Besides, if a man was meant to walk, why were horses made?

Cowboys never pretended to be perfect, but the simplicity of their lives and the decent standards of the code did produce men of high caliber. Tony put in more trail miles and saw more of the West than most old-timers, so I asked him about misfits, ill-tempered bullies like Joe's bronc-peeling older brother who enjoyed tormenting horses, women and kids. He answered, "Word got around and they couldn't get jobs. It was big country, but word got around."

It took a lot of men to work those big ranges—the cattle scattered to beat hell. What are ya gonna do? Ya can't have an army working for you year 'round.

J.K. Ralston

Kenny Trowbridge at work in the 1930s. Author's collection

Cow Chaperones

The ingenious ranch owner didn't need an army, he didn't even need a ranch. What he needed was a brand, a spot to put a chuck wagon on, a large herd of cattle and a group of eight or nine cowhands who worked for love, not money.

Tony Grace called the cowboy a cow chaperone. "With the old outfits, you better learn to handle cattle easy, keep 'em quiet. None of this yelling and running around like the movies show. Movies and western novels got it botched up badly. Keep 'em fat, conserve meat, that's the idea. They're being paid by the pound and they get paid off at the shipping point. Even if you weren't going to market, they just naturally believed in handling cattle as quiet as possible. We chaperoned those dogies."

Cow chaperones picked up cattle off the range for branding and castrating in the spring, and escorted cows to market in the fall. The head chaperone was called the ramrod, trail boss, wagon boss or cow foreman. When I escorted J.K. Ralston and another old hand and his wife to a St. Louis folk festival, J.K. referred to me as trail boss. I'd look over my shoulder as I hurried through the mazes of two big-city airports, wondering what to do if we missed connections. J.K., ambling along, carrying my leather purse (he was a frail eighty-six at the time, not able to carry his own suitcase). Tall and elegant in his gabardine western-cut suit, he would holler "It's okay, boss, we're holdin' up the rear."

Stories about camp cooks could fill another book, but there are few stories about bosses. There's not much to add to the facts: these men were tough, reliable, reasonable and smart. The boss needed a sense of humor to put up with the cowhands' practical jokes, and he had to lay down the law when jokes went too far. A bully didn't keep the job long enough to talk about.

"They had to be good men, and they had to be able to read men and cows," Tony said. "They couldn't just order men around like your average boss, couldn't say 'ya hafta do this or that.' They never demanded things of men they wouldn't do themselves, the old-timers just wouldn't take that. A good boss approached men in a nice manner, he showed respect."

"What about a boss who was bossy, or unfair?" I asked.

"He lost his crew," Tony replied.

Not that cowhands weren't willing to give a guy a chance. Folks compared Kenny Trowbridge to humorist Will Rogers; I asked Kenny if, like Will, he'd never met a man he didn't like and he replied, "Well, I wouldn't go that fur, but I never met a man I wouldn't give a chance."

The boss was given a fair chance, as were all the hands. A green cowhand could be educated by the other men, but if the boss proved to be a fool, the men would quit rather than bad-mouth him or the outfit.

Owners of outfits were seldom around, some living as far away as England or Scotland. Running the operation was usually left up to the boss. He had to know his way around big country—he decided where the crew would go to collect critters, where the cattle would be bedded down, and where the chuck wagon would make its next stop. He kept the books and divvied up the saddle horses so each new hand got a personal string.

Most hands didn't aspire to be boss, even though it paid up to $125 monthly, as compared to the thirty- to forty-dollar cowhand wage. Hands preferred being footloose and fancy-free, and being boss was big business.

Tom Harwood at Montana's annual fiddlers' meet, 1983. Photo by Jo Rainbolt

I'd met old hands, wranglers and cooks, but was wondering if the bosses had all died off young when I came across Tom Harwood.

Tom was legendary in the big sky country adjacent to northwestern Montana's Blackfeet Indian Reservation. He was a champion old-time fiddler, horse trainer, Blackfeet tribal elder, and he and his wife Ruby raised their own five kids and twenty foster children.

Tom's country lies east of the Rocky Mountain Front and runs all the way up to the Canadian border. It was big grass country when Tom was a boy, and even into the 1940s when his daughter Carma Adamson was riding horseback from one end to the other. Tom called Carma his cowhand. Born in Valier in 1930, she said the country of her childhood was all horse and cattle land with very little plowed under.

Tom was a Montanan, no doubt about that. His grandfather Thomas Harwood traveled west building forts for the U.S. Army during the Civil War, settled at Fort Benton along the Missouri in Montana Territory, started a trading post and married the daughter of a Blackfeet chief. Tom's dad was a top hand and a friend of western cowboy-artist Charles M. Russell. Many, many old hands claimed to have known Russell—always "Charlie" when they speak of him. (Joe Hughes said that he was the only surviving Montana cowhand who hadn't ridden with Russell: "I can't lie as good as a lot of these guys, so I never met him.") But in Tom's dad's case it was true. Tom's brother Paul even lived with the Russells in Great Falls.

Tom was a born cowboy. One of his earliest memories was of sitting on a corral fence at age four, watching his father and older brother brand the family's two milk cows after regular branding was over. It wasn't long after that when Tom took over the ranch chores, and became an expert hand in the kitchen. One thing led to another, until Tom became the youngest trail boss in Montana.

"I didn't pretend to be no bronc twister," he told me. "I rode a lotta horses, but I was a little better with a rope than I was with anything else. How'd I learn to rope? Well, it's just kinda natural. See there was eleven of us growing up, nine boys and two girls. The two older ones went to Carlisle Indian School, and Mark, he was the third one, he was kind of sickly. Anything went wrong, he got it. Somehow you couldn't kill me with a club, so the old man—he sorta relied on me. So I done all the chores around the ranch. That way I got quite a little practice roping, we had quite a few cattle, the folks did."

Still, Tom wanted to work for a big spread, like the Horseshoe Bar north of his parents' ranch, where Texas cattle were trailed up every two or three years, fattened on Montana grass and shipped to market.

"When I hired out they told me what day to be there. Was I just a kid? Yuh, I figure I was about nine. When I got there they didn't have no horse wrangler so [the ramrod] asked me could I wrangle horses and I said 'yuh.' He said a dollar a day, thirty a month.

After retiring from cowboying, Tony Grace didn't get too far away from horses when he ran a guest ranch in Jackson Hole, Wyoming in the 1930s. Courtesy Stan Grace

"So the next year when we got ready to go, he said, 'Tom, I promised you a cowboy job this year, but old Jimmy's sick and can't come out.' That was the cook, old Jim Winterberry. So Riley Sappo, that was his name, he was the ramrod of that outfit, he said, 'Suppose you can handle this chuck wagon for a coupla days or so until I get another man to take over?' I told him I supposed I could.

"Backing up to when I was a little kid, there was eight of us boys before there was a girl and when Mom was sick or on the brink, we hadda cook the meal. Old Paul, he never wanted to, and Mark, he was so durn slow he couldna got nothin' done anyhow, so it was either up to I or Bill. Anyway, we went out and it took [the boss] two and a half years to find another cook. Was I only ten when I started? Yuh, but I was a pretty good size, I was always big for my size."

By the time Tom was a teenager, he was a veteran with the Horseshoe Bar. "When I was sixteen or seventeen years old Riley had to quit. The owner came out there, stayed for about a week after old Riley left. Nobody was the boss, 'course we was down to just a few hands, being it was winter. One morning the owner said 'I'm gonna hafta tell ya somethin this morning. I'm gonna hafta put a man on here as ramrod…Tom has been here years. He's only a kid but the fact of the matter is, he knows the place better'n I do. I wonder if you boys could respect him and use a little courtesy towards him, he's the youngest one but I think he's the one that's capable.' So he put me in old Riley's place, there was two or three of 'em didn't like it very good. I stayed with the outfit 'til they quit the cattle business—let's see, that was four or five more years. Being trail boss was good, I kinda enjoyed it."

Wrangler at nine, boss at sixteen? Hard to swallow, but true. Given the chance, kids are amazing. Shortly after that conversation with Tom, I was visiting Art Wahl, and out of the blue he started talking about hauling passengers in a horse and cart from the depot to the hotel in the Norwegian town where he grew up. Knowing he left for the states at fifteen, I asked "How old were you when you ran this shuttle business?" He thought for a few moments and replied, "I think I was about eight—ya, I was eight." I didn't bat an eye. Other old-timers have told me similar stories of early responsibility. At age seven, Joe Hughes crawled on his belly through high grass to rope horses that were skittish with older hands, then rode them back to the Bitterroot Valley ranch of copper magnate Marcus Daly. After telling this, he pierced me with a serious gaze and said, "But don't make it seem like I was a cowboy at that age."

Tom's success as foreman can be explained in his attitude towards horses. "I think if you treat a horse right he treats you right. A lot of guys when they break a horse they beat 'em, they starve 'em, they believe in commandin' a horse all the time. I think it's the same with humans. If I tell you that you've got to do something, and you don't think you should, I think it's the wrong thing to do to you. But if we talk it over and we both decide on what would be the best way to do it, well that would be a lot better. That's the way you hafta handle the kids. Well, you hafta do it with everything."

On the opposite side of the job scale from the boss was the wrangler, usually a kid, hired for handling, grazing, watering and corraling the remuda. It annoyed J.K. that wrangler came to mean cowhand. "Wranglers didn't work cows!" he exclaimed.

For that very reason, wrangling wasn't sought after. A wrangler didn't work cows and he helped the cook, meaning he spent time afoot. However, it was a good place for a young fellow to learn the ropes. Veteran hands often had a soft spot for the kid trying to work his way from horse wrangler to real cowhand.

Between trail boss and wrangler was the cowhand. Fun-loving first of all, and generally hard-working, horse-loving, generous and always single. And appreciative of what J.K. called the pleasure of working for a well-run outfit.

A well-run outfit was simplicity itself—a hand was sent out to gather cattle, he had a certain area to cover (called a circle), and the details were up to him. In new country, a circle leader or the boss would drop one or two hands off in a certain area. "'Course a circle wasn't an exact circle, it covered the terrain. A circle had lots of jogs and jigs, Z's and S's and what have you," Tony explained as he sketched a roundup: chuck wagon in the center, circles extending out from it like wavy flower petals.

Trail rides were a different matter. Cattle were strung out in a long line, lead steers and riders in the front or point position, flank riders at the sides, weaker cattle and inexperienced hands in the back, riding drag. "Dust a problem? It was dusty all right, especially when you were riding drag. But we were too young to be bothered by little things like dust," Tony said.

Cowherding had to be hard work, but old-timers overlook the work part. When Tony described the easy Miles City hours, out at three a.m. and, if the work is done, back by three p.m., he didn't mention two-hour night guard and no-Sundays-off. When pressed about the work aspect, Tony laughed, "Yes, we put in some time all right, but we knew it was temporary. Winters were for sleepin'. Ya get a lot of rest holed up in a line cabin."

Art Wahl answered with more than one word when asked if herding cattle was hard work. "Nope. Lotsa jobs harder than that."

"Such as?" I prompted.

"Logging," he replied.

As a poet, J.K. described moments when a cowhand wonders why he chose such a life—the bone-weariness of night guard, the dreariness of a cold wet day. His poem about "Dayherding in the Rain," when "a minute seems a day," portrays the down side of things:

> I wish I had a cigaret, but with fingers stiff and dead,
> I couldn't roll one on a bet, and so I cuss instead.

His painting of the same title allows the viewer to share the misery, right down to the cowhand's dripping nose.

Joe referred to his chosen profession as the "lowest paid and hardest work on the job scale." In a poem, he put it this way:

> With the snakes and the lizards you slept on the ground,
> 'round through the worst blizzards for that forty and found.

(Forty referred to wages and found to the room and board, such as it was.)

Joe may have poked fun at his profession, but he wore his black felt cowboy hat and silk scarf till the last, and he pulled on his red-star boots until arthritis forced him into lace-ups. Joe was right, being a cowhand was often a lonely job, and he himself spent more than his share of frosty nights alone on the big prairie, camping without a crew or a chuck wagon. But in the process, he gained a reverence for the night sky and nature's daylight wonders greater than that of any other person I have known. Although it's seldom voiced, all old cowhands share this reverence—hours alone on horseback and in solo camps gave a man plenty of time for contemplation. A friend who packed mules and horses into wilderness areas for a decade and knew plenty of old hands called them *"roshis* on horseback." Zen masters indeed.

Old hands seem to take for granted phenomena the rest of us label "supernatural" or "mystical." More than one old hand has mentioned following a "certain feeling" and changing the outcome of a situation. Old-timers tend to think of themselves as creatures of the universe. Joe said that when you spend as many nights looking up at the big sky as he did, you become aware of all sorts of otherworldly happenings. He matter-of-factly told me about spotting balls of light sailing through the sky in eastern Montana's Bighorn River country in 1911, '12 and '13, and then finally seeing one land. Riding toward it, he saw it go straight up for about a hundred yards and take off to the east.

"If it woulda come my way, I hate to think what woulda happened to my cayuse. I'da had to ride him to death or quit him altogether and beat him back to the home ranch on foot," Joe laughed, then added, "'Course those balls of light had been seen by the Crows for generations. No mystery to them, they were the spirits of their ancestors, buried in those hills." Joe worked for a Crow rancher, Mark Real Bird; he learned the Crow language, participated in everday Crow life, and later wrote several stories about his experiences. Joe let few people read these finely-crafted, beautiful stories. He wrote them for himself. His feeling was that for a white man to publish intimate details of Native American lives would be showing a lack of respect. All the old hands voiced respect for the early Indian's "walk softly, put back what you use" lifestyle. To them, it was ideal. Even Art Wahl, who had left Norway to become a dime-novel cowboy and kill off savages, expressed anger at the American Indian's "sad deal."

In trying to describe the cowhand's true daily life, Joe never changed stories. I have come across two versions of the same experience, taped years apart, in which Joe described the same events almost word for word. Poems, however, were a different matter. With other poets' work, Joe exercised artistic license, changing lines and stanzas to "improve the work" or to "make it more real." But I recall one poem Joe left intact when he recited it for me,

"When There Wasn't Many Fences" by Bruce Kiscadden. The first stanzas describe the pleasures of a lone camp. The last two stanzas go:

> Yes, you like it on the roundup
> when the fellows laughs and jokes,
> But there's times a fellow feels better
> out away from other folks.
>
> There's no better place for thinking,
> though I couldn't tell you why
> Than to camp alone out somewhere
> and watch your campfire die.

Joe and I sat quietly when he finished. After a few minutes he said softly, "Just as real as doin' it."

Joe would have appreciated a poem by O'Malley I came across in an 1894 *Montana Stockgrowers Journal*. It reflects cowboy humor, as well as the accidental building of the myth. "The Cowboy Wishes" begins:

> I want to be a cowboy
> And with the cowboys stand,
> With leather chaps upon me
> And a six-gun in my hand.

O'Malley's cowboy, a "model puncher," longs for greenhorn trappings such as ornate saddles, silver-mounted bits, conchos big as dollars, silvered spurs, long rawhide reatas (lariats), big Colt forty-fives. The poem is hilarious to anyone who knows real cowhands. He expresses the wish to be macho—"I want to be a tough man, and be so very bad..."

The last two stanzas read:

> I want to be a buster
> And ride the bucking horse,
> And scratch him in the shoulders
> With my silvered spurs, of course.
> I'll rake him up and down the side,
> You bet I'll fan the breeze.
> I'll ride him with slick saddle
> And do it with great ease.
>
> I want to be a top man
> And work on the outside
> So I can ride within a herd
> And cut it high and wide.

Oh, a rep is what I want to be,
And a rep, you bet, I'll make.
At punching cows I know I'll shine;
I'm sure I'll take the cake.

Kenny Trowbridge, like most old hands, was an O'Malley fan. When I showed him a copy of "The Cowboy Wishes," he tilted back in his kitchen chair and laughed at almost every line. "That guy's been there. Ya know a rep like he mentions was the top hand, he'd ride out amongst roundup outfits looking fer his outfit's brand. A top job, hadda be a guy who really knew his way around, and O'Malley, he repped for the '79's, one of the biggest. He knew his stuff alright. Knew it enough to make fun of it."

Kenny scratched his full head of hair. "Trouble is," he bawled out, "seems like modern cowboys took O'Malley's spoofs serious, fer Crissake."

Only a fool argues with a skunk, a mule or a cook.
                                        Kenny Trowbridge

*Several large cow-camp Dutch ovens—
those essentials of chuckwagon cooking—are seen in this view of a worka-
day meal south of Twin Falls,
Nevada in the fall of 1919.
Courtesy of Tony Grace*

S.O.B. Stew and Sourdough

A cowhand's day began with the cook's call. "Come and git it!" was standard, but Cookie was just as likely to holler, "Roll out and bite the biscuit!" or "Bite the biscuit while she's hot!" or "Come and git it before I throw it on the ground!"

"And that's only the beginning…" yelled Kenny Trowbridge with his usual zeal. After he followed his chuck-wagon-cook father to Idaho at age fourteen, Kenny learned to ride when an old hand sent him out to look for a "mulie-cow with one horn" ("there ain't no such critter," Kenny explained), and spent his formative years tagging behind cattle and chuck wagons.

Kenny reminded me that cow camps were made up solely of men. "Dasn't repeat some of them wake-up calls for the general public. 'Come and git it or I'll spit in the skillet' is mild. Lemme see, Dad had a little poem, part of it went like this, 'Piss ants in the butter, flies in the meat, if you bastards are hungry get up here and eat'."

Cookie was one person in camp who could sulk or show signs of temperament, and he generally didn't hesitate to do so. It made sense to tread softly around Cookie, because food was one of the few pleasures on trail and a well-disposed cook usually made better vittles. A bucking bronc and rider might turn camp upside down, as illustrated in Charlie Russell's famous painting "Bronc to Breakfast," but such events were unplanned. The area around the chuck wagon was Cookie's territory and the men respected it. A hand wouldn't dream of tying his horse to a wagon wheel, or riding into camp in a cloud of dust (unless on a runaway bronc).

A man may have been his own boss on circle or trail, but the cook dictated the rules in camp. A hand always stopped a decent distance from the chuck wagon, dragging firewood behind his horse if he wanted a return favor (such as bread pudding or canned peaches) or if he just wanted to be in Cookie's good graces. He never used the chuck wagon lid for eating, it was the cook's working space. Men hunkered on the ground to eat. It was impolite to pass gas in the cook tent, especially in front of a hot cookstove. Beans were a staple, "breaking wind" jokes were common, and Kenny recalled a serious offender being beaten on the bottom with a pair of chaps.

Hands had lots of nicknames for the cook, names like Mom, Susie (derived from *cocinero*—co-seen-AIR-oh—Spanish for cook), Grub Spoiler, Dough Puncher or Old Lady. Kenny replied "Lord, no!" when asked if the cook was called such names to his face.

Tony Grace was good-natured, it ran in his family. "I like people, I like animals, I like everything. Father was that way, Mother very much so..." Taking up chuck wagon cooking didn't change him, but he knew he was an exception—"Cooks as a rule, I found 'em touchy."

A cook tried hard to live up to his cranky reputation, but he was not above barbering, doctoring and sometimes mothering the cowhand. Tony said no one criticized the cooking: "The next cook could be worse, or a hand could end up doing it himself."

Tony fell gently into do-

The chuckwagon is bathed in shade, but cowhands need to supply their own for this meal. Tony Grace is nearest the camera—his own small camera, being operated by a friend. Courtesy of Stan Grace

ing it himself, and ended up enjoying the art of slinging biscuits. "An out-fit I worked for needed a cook. I told the foreman I hadn't cooked in my life, didn't know a thing about it," Tony explained.

Tony's competence was written all over his well-worn face, and photo-graphs of him as a young hand show the same keen look. The foreman, no doubt an expert on faces, told Tony, "I know how to cook, I'll teach you."

"I kinda liked it," Tony found, "especially that kind of cooking. I was cooking for two or three men on a ranch. The boss showed me how to make yeast bread, and I got so I could make real good bread. In the winter when we got laid off I did some trapping that called for baching and cooking."

Kenny said a common saying around camp was "Only a fool argues with a skunk, a mule or a cook," but not all hands remember cooks as cranky. While describing first-day roundup bedlam, artist-poet J.K. Ralston said "...here's a new hand, got bucked off, somebody's tryin' to catch his horse. If the cook is like old Billy Woods he's hollerin' 'Catch him, catch him, I'll top him off for him' and he'd actually do that. He'd been a bronc rider..." In a poem about a sixty-two-year-old cook—"Lord of fryin' pan an' bowl"—J.K. describes how a horse injury retired a cowhand from the herding ground to the kitchen, which was often the case. J.K. writes from the cook's point of view:

> *...An' that's been nigh some twenty years or more.*
> *But here's the joke—I have to laugh!*
> *If I'd had any brains I'd had a job of cookin' long before!*

The poem relates the cook's pleasure at listening to raindrops in the tent while the cowhands shiver in a freezing rain, or cutting biscuits in the shade while the hands wilt.

> *A-cuttin' little biscuits,*
> *While the rest are brandin' calves,*
> *An' the sweatin' flankers labor in the sun.*
> *I'll peel a mess of taters*
> *An' cut 'em up in halves*
> *An' I'll roll a cigaret when this is done.*

Not all cooks had a tent for cutting biscuits, or shade for that matter. Tony went from cooking in a ranch kitchen in Montana to chuck wagon cooking in Arizona. "Here's my kitchen," he said, handing me a black and white photo picturing an expanse of desert disturbed only by a few cast iron cooking pots and a metal rod propped up by two more rods. Tony recalled starting supper under the chuck wagon when a storm came up.

"It was an awful rain," Tony said, "so I situated myself on my knees under the wagon, and started mixing biscuits on top of a fifty-pound sack of flour. Scraped a hole in the flour and put my water in there, and the proper amount of salt and baking powder, a little sugar—I always used a little sugar in 'em. I knew how much water to put in and made my biscuits right in that hole there. It held the water very well, absorbed only the amount of flour required. I can still the see the fellas standing around watching me. They were thinking they were gonna go hungry that evening, or probably have a real late supper."

Tony began cooking during fall roundup in 1913. He was a traveling cowboy, always ready to see new country, and that year he happened to be in the Southwest. A lot of men were looking for riding jobs, so when the chance came along to cook for the KM wagon, he took it. "I got to be a pretty fair hand with the Dutch oven—I like to cook, up to a point. Cowhands are easy, they don't dare complain and they like beef and biscuits three times a day. I wasn't long establishing a reputation in that part of the country. Lemme tell ya, the farther south ya go, the worse the grub gets. They cover it up with that red chili sauce."

Tony came to prefer cooking over riding while in Arizona. "I'll tell ya why. Two reasons. They didn't have big crews was number one, just Dutch oven outfits, eight or ten men. You could put a meal together in a hurry. Didn't have to set tables or anything, they take a tin plate and eat right out of the pot. All you gotta do is prepare it, line it up and say 'Come and get it,' they'll come and get it. Second reason for cooking was they were the poorest mounted cowboys I ever saw, small horses and few of 'em. I came from Miles City where they had unlimited numbers of big horses. Riding those little ponies didn't look too good to me. Cooking paid twenty-five dollars a month more, too, and there was always a job waiting for a good cook, seems like."

Tony the good-natured cook even made cream puffs for the hands, his own concoction of pastry dough, canned milk, sugar and eggs. Eggs in camp were scarce as hen's teeth, but easily traded for beef if there were farmers in the area. All wagons carried a case of canned milk, and Wisconsin-born Tony lamented the lack of fresh milk, "surrounded by millions of cows and no milk."

Tony did whatever needed to done, including haircuts. "Usually there was a pair of dull scissors around. The first one I barbered was north of Billings on a ranch that had a post office, and in the post office was a little pair of shears they used to cut the cord on packages. You know how sharp they'd be. The fella looked like a beaver'd been chewing on the back of his head, but he took it good-naturedly."

In looking after the health of his outfit, the cook was more or less a medicine man, running on faith and homemade remedies. "Lemme think," bellowed Kenny Trowbridge, scratching his full head of steel-gray hair, trying to recall the medical secrets of his father, "Dad used a lotta flour, stopped cuts from bleeding fer horses and men. Make a paste outa it. He'd slap fresh cow manure and puffballs fer bad cuts on horses. Fer medicine he had along a few things, blue vitr'ol, slack lime, a bottle of turpentine, a gallon o' castor oil."

Although Tony had the old-timer's "nuthin' to it" attitude, he admitted that the work was never done for a cook. "Mom" was a fitting title. Cooking was the easy part, But also there was water to pack from a creek or river, firewood to collect and cut, fires to build and meals to clean up after. All this work might be considered reasonable if camp were permanent, as in a logging camp, but during roundup the cook had to move his kitchen up to three and four times a day.

Moving a chuck wagon is not a simple matter; Cookie needed to be a teamster along with his other skills. Getting a chuck wagon out of a mud hole was tougher than roping out a bogged cow. Small wonder Cookie was often crabby, although Tony said "getting up so darn early" contributed most to the cook's ornery state of mind.

Old-timers recall pre-dawn pan-clanging and shuffling, even singing and whistling—anything to keep the cook from being the only man awake at such a deadly hour. Kenny said the cook often woke the men with glee, more than willing to share the early-morning hours with an exhausted crew.

Hands slept on the ground. Some might throw together old "soogans" (quilts) for a bedroll, but most were like Tony and used wool blankets and good-quality canvas, creating a waterproof and toasty cocoon. Tony said the morning ritual went like this—"You'd hear the cook's call, first thing you'd reach for was papers and a sack of Bull Durham, light that. Old hands didn't chew, they rolled their own. Then you'd reach over and get your hat, put that on, get your boots and put them on. Never took your shirt off and slept in long johns all year round, so pants was the last thing you put on. Hard to put on over boots? No, we generally had small feet and our boots fit like gloves, made for riding, not walking."

Kenny was a natural storyteller and cowboy historian, but he was a young fellow in his mid-seventies, and he enjoyed hearing Tony's tales from earlier days when the three of us got together. Kenny's big amiable face lit up when he heard Tony's early-morning-ritual description.

"Jes' like in the bunkhouse! Goddam, I can jes' see the fellas runnin' around in shirts and cowboy hats, lookin' for their goddam Levi's!"

Tony and Kenny provided a complete description of the chuck wagon, a small self-contained ship afloat on the prairie. It was an ordinary lumber wagon with a mess box set in the rear, where everything necessary for survival was stashed. Inside the wagon were cubbyholes that held staples such as salt, sugar and flour, and the cook's doctoring potions—blue vitriol, slack lime, castor oil and a bottle of medicinal liquor (carefully guarded). A rawhide compartment or boot attached under the wagon held Dutch ovens and pans. There was usually room inside the wagon to throw bedrolls and the cowhands' possessions, each man's kept to a minimum and stored in a grain bag called a "war bag." Large outfits might use a second open wagon to store bedrolls and war bags. J.K. Ralston said the bedroll wagon for big outfits would be piled so high it made a hay wagon look small. Cooks for big outfits had a helper, called a flunkie, to drive the second wagon and help with chores.

The back lid of the chuck wagon had a folding leg attached so that so that the cook's work table was formed when the leg was lowered. While no hand dared eat from it, Tony laughed, "I left a can of honey on that table and came back from fetching water to find two *horses* eating it. Galier and Papoose. Galier was probably the one upset it, he was really smart, and gentle. Somewhere I got a picture of me standing on his back, gentle as could be."

"What were horses doing wandering around camp?" I asked, knowing by this time horses were kept in a rope corral.

"Oh, he was a little small to put in a regular string so we kept him around camp, sorta like a pet, fed him biscuits and hotcakes…" and Tony related a hilarious incident featuring Galier and himself playing a round-the-wagon game over a biscuit—with the horse outsmarting the cook.

Tony said favorite horses were often retired early, so they wouldn't wear out, and given free rein around camp. Some cooks regarded these pets as nuisances, but Tony welcomed them.

Tony got excited when I showed him a copy of Charlie Russell's "Bronc to Breakfast" painting. "…That chuck wagon is the perfect picture of the old-time wagon. This whole picture is good, angora chaps and the cook looks all right. He's wearing a vest—they used to all wear vests. And white shirts—the hands all wore white shirts. Russell gets it right down to the wrinkle in the boot. There's a pretty big crew on his painting, big outfit. Biggest roundup outfit was Pumpkin Creek Pool, the year I was with them they had as many as forty men at times. If you have forty men scattered around a wagon eating they'd cover quite a bit of territory."

Feeding cowhands wasn't difficult because they didn't mind the same fare day after day. One of two breakfasts was usually served—fried steak with biscuits and gravy, or fried steak and hotcakes. Strong black coffee was the life blood of the camp, and so a cook who kept a pot going for night guard was almost revered. Sometimes the only words exchanged at breakfast were "man at the pot," an offer to pour second or third cups.

The cowhand's purported recipe for making coffee was simple—boil two pounds of coffee in two gallons of water for two hours, throw in a horseshoe and if it sinks, the coffee isn't done yet. Old hands generally gave up smoking when their youthful riding days were over, but they kept the "strong and black" coffee habit, referring to restaurant coffee as "dishwater" or "belly-wash."

Tony Grace in his field kitchen. Courtesy of Stan Grace

Joe Hughes said some early ranches were owned by tea-drinking Englishmen and that cowboys made fun of the tea-drinkers. Joe gave up coffee in his eighties and had a hard time switching to tea. He said earlier teabags had been made from cotton and even modern tea tasted like cloth to him.

The noon meal was another big feed. After breakfast and clean-up, while the cowhands groped for their horses in a rope corral in the half-dark, the cook would start a roast simmering in the Dutch oven. Old hands claim there's nothing better than a hunk of beef slow-cooked over the coals.

A Dutch oven is a huge deep cast iron skillet with a heavy lid on top and three legs under the bottom. It was the essential piece of equipment for the chuck wagon cook. He heaped coals around it and used it to bake savory biscuits and roasts, he fried steak in it and boiled beans and made puddings and fruit stews. He could even be cajoled into using it for deep-frying doughnuts.

When Kenny Trowbridge was a featured storyteller at the Jefferson Expansion Memorial Museum in St. Louis, the authenticity of the Old West displays impressed him, until he spied the Dutch oven by a chuck wagon. "Jes' look at that piddlin' thing! Be lucky to feed two men outa it, never mind a crew!"

Tom Harwood, who exemplified the cowhand's "nuthin' to it" attitude, had thirty men to feed for the Horseshoe Bar ranch. "It wasn't so bad," he said. "We used what you call Dutch ovens. Get that kettle boiling with meat or beans or dried fruit, then I'd get orders to move camp maybe ten miles or so. I'd let that old Dutch oven boil to the last minute, cuz the stove was always the last thing to move. We'd set the kettle in this metal-lined box in the chuck wagon and lotta times it'd keep right on boilin'. I'd go over to the next camp and set up the stove [a crossbar kitchen, Tony's style] and, by golly, the beans'd still be bubblin' away. That cast iron was thick, ya know."

While his "temporary" cooking job lasted two and a half years, Tom said, "I got in quite a lot of slinging biscuits there."

Biscuits ranked next to beef and coffee in the cowhand's affections and were given pet names such as dough gods and sinkers. "When I first started out I made my biscuits kinda small, but I got wise to that," Tom said. "Some guy with dirty hands be reachin' in there every minute for another biscuit so I got to makin' em bigger'n that ashtray there, so about one biscuit'd do him. I always had what we called a bread can, Chase and Sanborn coffee used to come in it. I'd cook up a few biscuits ahead a time, then if I hadda move the chuck wagon I always had a canful o' biscuits."

Many cooks made their biscuits with sourdough. Kenny's dad insisted that baking powder and soda were bad for a person and always used yeasty sourdough for leavening.

Sourdough was regarded with affection. Bachelor cowboys and old-time cooks and miners were fondly referred to as sourdoughs. Kenny recalled his father taking his crock of sourdough into his bedroll to keep it from freezing on cold nights. With his Dutch oven and sourdough he created bread, cake, biscuits, even pie crusts. Whenever a cowhand shot a Franklin grouse ("easy ta do," Kenny drawled, "they're so damn dumb."), Kenny's dad would parboil it and serve it up with sourdough dumplings. Dumplings were such a cowboy favorite that Kenny's dad called flour "dumpling dust."

Some Montana sourdough starters are a century old, nursed along from those begun by miners and cowboys in the late 1800s. Starter is simple to make. Nothing to it. Soak a tablespoon of yeast in warm water, add a teaspoon of sugar and enough flour to make a thick batter. Place the mixture in a stoneware, enamel or glass pot and cover, allow to stand until it bubbles and ferments, at least two days. Stir occasionally and add more flour or water if needed. Sourdough gives baked goods a distinctive, tangy flavor. When starter is taken out, more flour and water should be added to keep it going. Don't let it freeze (take it to bed on cold nights).

A more complicated cowboy favorite is S.O.B. stew, referred to as Son of a Gun stew in mixed company. Tony and Kenny chuckled at the squeamishness of observers when some old-timers tried to relive the past by building an S.O.B. stew at a Montana picnic. The ingredients are the innards of a freshly slaughtered young beef. The stew is heavy on marrow gut, the tube connecting the cow's two stomachs; supposedly delicious, marrow gut is used by the foot in old-time recipes.

Marrow gut must come from an undisturbed animal since undigested food particles in it would ruin the stew. Tony and Kenny gave almost identical recipes for S.O.B. stew and both mentioned it was the only dish in which a cowboy would eat kidneys. Marrow gut was cut into small pieces, dredged in flour, seasoned with salt and pepper, then fried in beef suet or lard until crisp (in a Dutch oven, of course.) Next the cook chopped up heart, brains, liver, sweetbreads (pancreas of a calf) and kidneys, and threw it all in the Dutch oven to simmer in boiling water with the marrow gut.

Old-timers prefer steak well done, scoff at mushrooms and leaf lettuce as "exotic" and wouldn't dream of eating Oriental or even Italian food (they will eat rice sweetened in a pudding or an occasional spaghetti and meatball meal.) And what's their unanimous choice for a mouth-watering meal? S.O.B. stew, a meal that calls for ingredients usually sampled by only the most sophisticated diners.

"Pretty weird food for a cowboy. I know why you old hands like it so much, because it's all-beef," I told Tony.

"It's *delicious*—but the beef part is valid. Cowboys wanted it three times a day. I've eaten enough to fuel a dozen turbines. You need that fat when you work hard, your body uses it for fuel," Tony replied. Whatever the reason—hard work, fresh air, good beef, sunny disposition—Tony was still amazing at ninety-six.

My old hands teased me for my preference for "rabbit feed." They cared little for vegetables beyond spuds, corn and dried beans, but they did like dried fruit. Dried fruit came in twenty-five–pound wooden crates and was a staple with all good outfits. Cooks stretched their imaginations with dried fruit. Kenny recalled his dad using dried apples, prunes, apricots and peaches in cobblers, turnovers, puddings and pies (the crust was usually biscuit dough but hands were still delighted). Prune jokes were common; for instance, cowhands claimed the man saving up the most prune pits would get the sought-after winter jobs. The significance is beyond me, and even Kenny claimed to have forgotten the meaning.

Eggs were a rarity, and to be enjoyed when available. Cowhands were known to order up to a dozen fried eggs in a sitting during their infrequent trips to town (and suffer because of it). Hands wanted theirs fried over easy, and said the cook who broke a yolk "shipwrecked an egg." (Tony recalled an Arizona cook called Shipwreck Bill.) Eggless puddings were common for dessert. Tony said it was common for a cowhand confined in camp because of injury to persuade the cook to make everybody's favorite, Son of a Gun in a Sack. Chopped suet was mixed with flour, raisins (or other chopped dried fruit) and water to form a heavy dough. The dough was put into an empty cloth sugar or salt sack and boiled an hour. A sweet sauce was usually mixed up to top the pudding. Sucamagrowl was another favorite—a pudding made from sugar, water, vinegar, flour and cinnamon with bits of biscuit dough floating in it.

"All these goodies, are you sure the cook's cranky reputation wasn't played up?" I asked.

"Nope, every time Charlie Russell met one he wondered if the guy was human. Cheezus, a cook'd even throw water under the chuck wagon, didn't want no hand takin' a nap in the shade under his wagon," Kenny said.

Kenny knew a hilarious song, "Boomer Johnson," about a ranch cook so ornery he put his six-shooter through his inedible doughnuts and made the hands eat them. Finally one of the hands had enough and shot the cook dead.

A cook who finally fell into disfavor with the crew might not get killed, but he was in trouble. Tony recalled an incident where camp was set up near a farm in Arizona and a hog got into the cooking pot. The cook, a sneaky sort with dirty fingernails (cowhands liked their cooks clean) put he lid back on the pot as if nothing had happened. A cowhand recuperating in camp (there always seemed to be one) warned the men and the stew wasn't touched. Tony didn't elaborate, but said the hands "made life pretty miserable for that bird that night and the next morning he quit."

A cook might be catered to in camp, but in town he was one of the guys. Tony recalled Sourdough Jack, a roundup cook who liked whiskey. "Jack tended to be quite crabby, a young man but not the easiest man to get along with. If a man is inclined to be a little ornery give him a few drinks too many and it'll show." Jack had those few too many in the White Saloon in Miles City and stared baiting a hand who was talking to the owner, Smith White. Most cowhands were of slight build, but Tony recalled this one as big and good-natured with a fist like a ham. "The fella's name was Lloyd, he loved ridin' buckin' horses, a regular riding machine."

Tony said it was quite humorous, Jack kept coming behind Lloyd and taking him by the shoulder, saying, in Tony's words, "Turn around, you so and so, I'm gonna whip you." Lloyd just shrugged him off. Finally he tired of it, turned around and decked Jack, knocking him cold.

Cooks got away with a lot in camp, but truly bad ones suffered the same fate as misfit cowhands. Word got around and the cook couldn't find work. Donovan McGee remembers his favorite cow foreman, Old Man Nation, making it impossible for a terrible cook called Cooty Slim to work the chuck wagon circuit. "Old Nation said, 'You can hire out for a dude outfit, but if I ever hear you hiring out for a cow outfit—I'll look you up'."

Don grinned in his Irish way, "He didn't say what he'd do."

...the sound of a harmonica could set us off.

Tony Grace

Tony Grace saved this postcard view of riders young and old in Miles City before World War I, when the town was his home base.

"I'm a Wolf, but I'm a Tame One"

Tony Grace and Art Wahl worked around Miles City for different outfits in 1910. They got together more than seventy years later at a puncher's picnic in Kenny and Verna Trowbridge's tree-shaded yard. Joe Hughes was there, too, along with some younger hands. Joe was listening to fiddle music and eating ice cream while Tony and Art were sitting in the shade and looking at each other's faces, trying to figure out if they'd seen each other in 1910.

The two former Miles City cowboys didn't talk much. I did overhear Tony ask Art, "You with those C-K boys shot out those railroad lights?"

"Nope," Art replied.

Driving Tony and Viola home, I asked Tony about the shooting incident. I can't recall his exact reply, something about shooting out street lights and signs was okay, but those C-K boys overstepped bounds when they went to the railway station.

The next time I talked cowboys with Tony, the subject of hell-raising came up. "Lonesomeness accounted for a lot of it. You just don't know until you've lived that way how you feel after being out away from people for maybe a year or six months. Spring and fall, generally beef shipping time in the fall, was the only time they got to town. After you've been out like that, you get in town and hear a little music, somebody play a mouth harp and it sounded like a brass band."

"No guitars in camp? Or harmonicas?" I asked. Somewhere in my memory bank was a picture of a cowboy singing and playing by firelight.

"Very seldom. No room. We only took what we could carry in a grain sack, sometimes we could stash an item in a box below the chuck wagon. No frills on the trail, that's why even a small cowtown looked mighty good to us. You were right up on your toes, ready for anything and everything. There's some of this stuff comes into these dime novels, exaggerated, too."

J.K. said the only music on the trail was an occasional harmonica. "I can only tell you what I saw, space was [at] a premium and I never saw any in-

The author's sketch of some of her cowboy friends reminiscing in 1983 during a picnic in Verna and Kenny Trowbridge's back yard. Gathered in Darby that day were, left to right, Kenny Trowbridge, Joe Hughes, Tony Grace and Art Wahl.

struments on trail. Later days, way later, after World War One, the Frye outfit had a cook who was a damn good musician and he carried his banjo all the time." The image of the Hollywood-cowboy strumming a guitar by the camp-fire had been put to rest.

Old-timers tell stories. They seldom generalize. As Kenny Trowbridge said, "It was damn hard fer me to believe at first that anybody's interested. Hell, we lived it, we didn't think, 'Ain't this unusual...' In a way, I still live it, what happened back then interests me a helluva lot more than what's happenin' today."

Tony sensed the difficulty of trying to write about a culture and a time that wasn't mine. He explained things to me. For instance, I figured from the hell-raising talk that this was one point where Hollywood myth merged with reality. But it didn't work that way, not quite.

"If you judge by what you see in the movies, you get the picture wrong," Tony explained. "What'd ya see? Cowboys spending days in the saloon, drinkin' and fightin' and shootin'. That's so far from the truth it's pathetic. The ranches were lonesome places, very quiet. There wasn't much excitement on a ranch. Handling rough stock, breaking horses, you had that kind of excitement, otherwise they were very quiet places to be." Spring and fall roundups meant time away from the ranch, but roundups meant business. "Night before the roundup, stagger into camp, put away the poker chips, forget about the girls, from now until the cattle are shipped it's all business," J.K. Ralston said.

But away from the quietness of the ranch and the demands of chaperoning wild-eyed critters on trail, cowpunchers went temporarily crazy. Mostly he shot into the air, but a cowhand could show off his talent with a gun by shooting the dot off an "I" in a sign, and leave it to his boss to make amends.

"We don't have any ways to let off steam in modern society. That probably explains a lot of the violence and vandalism," I said to Tony. "Look at primitive societies, they all had some sort of dance or ritual for going berserk. You fellows were probably a lot easier to get along with in camp because you could look forward to being crazy in town."

Tony approved of my theory.

Joe said cattle-shipping towns arranged to have deputies on duty when wagons camped nearby. "That way when a guy got a little bit glorious they could haul him back to the wagon. The wagons would only be there a few days 'til they got the cattle all loaded, train loaded up, so it wasn't asking too much of the deputies."

The real fun started when different outfits hit the same town at the same time. "The guys would have a lot of fun, they raised so much hell around town that deputies made it a rule only one wagon in town at a time."

Joe related a hilarious incident between two wagons ("wagon" is the term for an outfit) that happened before the "one wagon" rule was in effect. I never asked Joe the name of the town.

"I wasn't there this time, I guess maybe they shot things up a little, but not with firearms. One of the guys told me they got into kind of a fuss between the two outfits and one of 'em took one side of the street and the other across the street and they got to throwin' all the eggs the stores had. Throwed 'em at one another across the street. Plastered the town up pretty bad, I guess." (It's funny that cowboys would abuse that many eggs since they were so treasured and rare on trail.)

Joe wasn't present at the egg-throwing party, but he did his share of living it up. The first time Joe ran away, he got a ranch job in his home county—until a deputy warned him to move on since Joe's ornery Irish father wanted him back. Joe and a cowhand buddy, both about seventeen, decided to go north to the Flathead Valley in the Mission Mountains and help round up the last of the buffalo. They got "oiled up" before the train left the station and, after boarding, threw their saddles on adjoining seats and immediately fell asleep. Trouble was, they'd boarded the wrong train and were headed east instead of north. It took Joe a while to pay his way to eastern Montana's grasslands, where he finally worked as a cowboy. "I guess I was officially a cowboy, doing the same work I'd always done and almost gettin' paid for it."

Nobody told more colorful stories than Joe, although it took perseverance on my part; Joe was a stickler for getting it right. And the only reason Joe went along with my story-hunger was to make me happy. I usually dropped in on the spur of the moment, minus a tape recorder. We'd start off with a sip of wine or a cup of tea and some good laughs. Joe's wry Irish humor hit me just right. A word or a phrase or a chuckle jogged his storehouse of poems and he'd recite one; "They keep comin' back, tellin' how it was better'n anything," he once said.

A story would usually follow. I'd jot lines in my appointment book, on a napkin, or on the borders of old papers. My experience as a newspaper reporter allowed me to take rapid and accurate notes, although Joe questioned my accuracy.

"Joe," I'd say, "if we wrote things your way nothing would ever get done. Ever. Now have I ever misquoted you?"

"Well, I told you about the time you put me with the wrong outfit, anybody who read it would make me out a liar."

The incident I had written about took place in 1910, so I wasn't too concerned about Joe's reputation.

He'd laugh, "I dunno, I just dunno about you and your knack for bringin' 'em back. Sure you're not one of them hypnotists?"

Joe was the gentlest of men. He seldom used swear words, his voice was soft, he laughed often. He never lost his good looks, he just got craggier and less like Rudolph Valentino as he aged. I can't imagine him conceited (he wasn't) but I have no problem picturing him young and "glorious" on a trip to town.

This is storytelling, Joe-Hughes–style, where one thing leads to another.

"Did I get up glorious and uproarious in town? Well, I got pretty uproarious when I thought somebody had stole my coat. It was the first time I got money to buy a coat, a good wool mackinaw, I was needin' it for the winter anyway."

"Besides just wanting it, right?"

One kind of trip to town worth dressing up for was when hands went to Chicago to show cavalry horses to European buyers before the Big War. Tony Grace at center. Courtesy of Stan Grace

"Right. It was too warm to wear in the evenin.' I left it in the bull tent. It got chilly a little later and was just about dark when I went back for it. On the way back I passed sort of a comical team. A big guy, Collier was his name, he had been with the outfit for a long time. Well, he was layin' off to the side of the [wooden] sidewalk which went out of town a ways. He was layin' kinda in the gutter and it was starting to spit rain—that's another reason I needed my coat…It was raining, and he was layin' on his back kinda rollin' around, didn't give a getup. But I helped him up and he was cussin' everything and everybody. I said, 'What's the matter, Collier, what the hell's the matter with you, what you cussin' about?' He said, 'Well, some son of a B is pissin' in my face."

Joe leaned into his tea cup with laughter, and even his bushy eyebrows were shaking. He almost never used off-color expressions around "ladies."

"See what happens when you get me goin' on these old times?"

Joe and I brought out the laughter in each other. After we'd stopped laughing over that incident, I asked him what became of his jacket.

"Got back to the wagon, went to get my coat and the coat was gone. Boy, I was kinda mad, and I figured what the devil? The cook was there, I went in the chuck wagon and asked him. He said, 'Well, there's been some of the boys around, getting slickers and things for the rain and went back to town.' He didn't know but didn't think anybody wore it away. I decided somebody musta stolen my coat. Cook didn't seem wise to what had really happened—I dunno, he mighta been, I forget. Anyway, I went back to town without it, I did. Figured I was gonna catch somebody with my gun and make him dance for it. If I woulda met somebody with the same kinda coat, I'da been in trouble. When I got back to the wagon, it was in the jockey box, under the wagon where we kept things. I guess they just took it to see what I'd do."

"Well, you got mad, and you're slow to anger, aren't you, Joe?"

"Oh, yuh, it takes somethin' to anger me, but that coat cost me a month's wages."

Most old punchers played poker. Joe recalled sitting up all night with another young cowhand in a fleabag hotel, throwing chips and playing poker across a narrow bed and taking turns reciting verses of Robert Service's "The Shooting of Dan McGrew." Seventy years later, Joe recalled every verse of that very long poem. If the old hands I've met are a fair poll, Service was the cowhand's favorite poet. He didn't write about cowboys and the West, but his poetry about the Yukon appealed to cowhands. Service wrote about real people—miners, bartenders, ladies of the evening.

Joe said all the good action took place in the old-time saloons. A man could recite a poem, belt out a tune, order drinks for the house, dance a jig. Joe recalled a buddy who got so carried away in a saloon during cattle-shipping time that he waved his six-shooter and hollered "I'm a wolf!" Noticing a deputy directly behind his left shoulder, he added meekly, "But I'm a tame one."

Joe lamented the passing of the old-time bars, claiming the jukebox was the "ruination of it all." Joe was recalling a lot of poems to me one summer night in our Bitterroot Valley town of Hamilton in southwestern Montana. I asked if he had a favorite and he replied, "One of my favorites, really, has to do with the old saloons, maybe because I could always get a good drink. A guy in Helena maybe forty, fifty years ago said he wrote it, but, hell, he wasn't even as old I was. I don't think he did. I knew it before he was born, if I ain't too rattle-headed to remember, because it's pretty long."

Joe did remember, and I had along my tape recorder. He called the poem "What's Yours, Pard?" and couldn't identify the author, but I've since learned it was "Shorty's Saloon" by John B. Ritch. It started out melancholy:

By the trails in the pass on the plains of nowhere,

Stood Shorty's saloon, but now it's not there.

The poem described the click of poker chips, violins playing and the general merriment of cowboys drinking, dancing, singing, "I'm just a poor cowboy and I know I've done wrong."

By the last verse, I could see why it was Joe's favorite. The poet must have been a fellow like Joe, one of those who knows time brings changes.

...And the story of those who lived through the change

Of the wild free life of the borderless range.

The poem ended with old Shorty looking out of the mist and asking "What's yours, pard?"

Joe stood up, said "I'll take a drink to that," and dug for a special-occasion bottle of whiskey. "I wonder if there ain't a little bit of tap left in this."

He poured us both a shot. "Cheers. Here's to you and me and old Shorty," I said, adding, "You know any cowboy toasts, Joe?"

Joe cleared his throat and lifted his glass.

Here's to the bronc what throwed me so high

That my backbone's hurt from the deep blue sky.

Here's to old earth where I lit when I fell

Come down from the heaven like a bat outa ...

He grinned, embarrassed that he'd almost cussed in front of a lady, even a lady who drank Wild Turkey with him. "Well, there it is, I reckon. When I get talkin' cowboy language I'm apt to get into almost anything."

I grinned back. Later when I played the tape back for Joe I could almost hear us grinning. "You guys must have had some pretty creative toasts," I said when I turned off the recording.

"You're tellin' me," Joe replied in a way that let me know I hadn't heard nuthin'.

Kenny-the-storyteller couldn't come up with any toasts "fit fer public consumption," but thought Tony Grace might know some half-way presentable ones.

Tony, with the gift of total recall, handily came out with this little beauty:

Here's to those who wish us well

Those who don't can go to hell.

He and Viola insisted I have a piece of pound cake with strawberries and a glass of fruity red wine for the next toast:

I drink to your health when I'm with you.

I drink to your health when I'm alone.
I drink to your health so much
I'm about to lose my own.

"Wanna hear a cold-blooded toast?" Tony asked. And of course I did.

Here's that we may grow fat
On the beef that grew fat on the grass
That grew on the graves of those who did not like us.

Both Tony and J.K. Ralston's toasts should be heard to be appreciated. They boomed them out in expressive, resonant tones. J.K. recited the most poetic toast:

From out earth's dusty old corral where failures press
May every bronco that you rope be named success.
May raging blizzards miss thy range and pass thee o'er
And troubled northers ne'r pile drifts around thy door.
And when at night you camp, may it chance to pass
You find yourself on peaceful creek near good grass.
And when the final roundup comes some autumn day
May your mark upon the book of books be this—
Okay.

J.K. said cowboys didn't just drink and toast and shoot up towns for entertainment. They danced. "In those days they had the most beautiful waltzes. Do you know how to waltz? Isn't that the finest dance there is? You've gotta have a good slick floor to do it right. It's a shame they hadda get into all this other business because the waltz and the two-step and the three-step and all those dances we used to do, they were the good dances. And the McGitty we used to do—that was different than the schottische—and the flirtation polka. See, I learned those right in cow country at dances at ranches, not in dance halls at all."

A cowhand didn't spend all his life on roundup. Many hands spent off-season time working out of a bunkhouse, and for them, Saturday night meant dances. Many dances were held at country schoolhouses, and the whole community showed up. Mary Welte of Hamilton, who grew up in north-central Montana, recalled starting out from the family's homestead when the sun was high and getting to the dance just about dark. Mary knew about dances, having played in an old-time dance band into her eighties. And she knew about cowboys, having married one.

"Saturday night was whoop 'em up time for the cowboy," she said. "They'd go to a dance in their very best bibs and tuckers. They all had saddle horses, they'd tie them in the shade of the schoolhouse, or if there was a barn at the schoolhouse, they'd put 'em out there tied to wagon wheels.

They didn't dance like now: in between one dance and another these days the girl playing the piano hardly turns the page and they start up again. They used to promenade 'round before the music started in again, the guy that was blowing the harmonica couldn't stand it that much. These dances went on all night, and they had a big supper.

"Before they headed home in the morning, the very last thing the cowboys would do was they'd all get on their horses and whoop it up and shoot their six-shooters in the air and make a helluva lotta noise. Why, I don't know, but I've been through it a lot and the horses that were teams didn't like it and they'd try to run away from us, so we had quite a time handling the team. We always knew the cowboys were gonna do it, so whoever was handling the team was holding on to the lines pretty good."

J.K. had a story about one of the more elaborate productions, and how bad weather wouldn't stop such festivities. In 1905, his father, Will, had put together a beautiful cow outfit west of Culbertson in eastern Montana for a wealthy Helena family, the Tatums. This outfit, called the Capital P, was located across the Missouri River from the small town of Brockton, and had two complete ranches and five permanent cow camps (each camp with a cabin for cowboys and shed and corrals for horses). Will Ralston managed the whole setup; his family lived on one of the ranches and called that the home ranch.

Probably the best part of the whole set-up, according to J.K., was the living room at the home ranch. "The ranch my father managed had a great big cottonwood log house and it was known all over the country because it had a huge living room, twenty-six feet long—actually it was a dining room—and people were always devilin' my mother to throw dances. So before the fall roundup my mother decided to throw a dance, and a big one."

A fiddle was often the sole instrument at a dance, but not at this one. "We had a couple coming up from Culbertson with horns and a gal named Inez Parmer was comin' over to play the piano. Our piano was still in Helena and old Homer Armstrong was gonna bring over his piano that he had for his girls. We were gonna have some damn good music for this dance."

People came from thirty miles around, quite a distance in horse and buggy days. "The damn rain come on and just poured. People came up from Culbertson on the train and Henry Miller went down to Brockton and brought 'em across the Missouri River with a rowboat, brought to the ranch in a spring wagon in the pouring down rain. It was about six miles from the river to the home ranch. A man, Butler was his name—top man with the HS—he and his wife had a top buggy and came down in that buggy.

"Fred Sullivan, who in later days became a sheriff in our part of the coun-

Art Wahl astride Goldie, the horse he trained to step into his own Missoula tavern. Art's wife Bert stands to his left. Old hands never forgot a horse, and Goldie's full name of Highland Gold, along with those of Kelly and Flicka beside her, are carefully noted on this family snapshot. Courtesy of Astrid Wahl Batchelder

try, was a horse man at this time and had his sister-in-law visiting, and brought her and his wife and his kids, puts 'em all in a spring wagon. Tipped over in the mud about five miles from the ranch, scrambled their cakes and everything. In those days everybody brought something, it was standard procedure on the range. If it was early spring or wintertime they'd bring hay for their horses."

J.K. paused in his recollection to chuckle at the rain and the havoc it created. "Everything was soaking wet, slippery. Floyd Davis was riding one of these broncs, you know how a bronc is, afraid of everything, always off to one side. He didn't get far enough over to the right and he rode off the cut bank into the night. Cut a big gash under his cheekbone but otherwise neither him or the horse got hurt. He could ride the same horse the rest of the way. Homer started out with the piano, got about five miles out on the road and tipped the piano over, that was the end of that. So we didn't have any piano but the horns got there and a coupla fellas with a violin and a guitar. So we danced the whole night long, then fed anybody who had to go any distance in the morning."

J.K. paused, smiled and looked around. "I was ten years old and I remember it well."

J.K.'s eyes were still dreamy, he wasn't finished with the dance. "They danced 'til daylight, that was the old ranch tradition. I'll never forget the picture ya see, here's comin' daylight and you look out the window and you see the horses tied along the corrals. And always some horse is loose, a horse has kicked at him or something and he's reared back and broke his rope. I never saw a dance yet that didn't take a rider or two to go round up the horses that's broken loose."

A few moments of silence, and one more recollection. "'Home Sweet Home' was always the last dance, that was standard. I've seen more than one cowboy have on his chaps, get out there and mount his horse, and have to come back in for that last dance."

Sure it was a hard life, but we didn't know it.

Mary Graves Welte

Joe and Pearl Hughes in the days they were leaving notes for each other in their "Rose Garden Post Office." Author's collection

The Rose Garden Post Office

Only a woman could lure a cowhand off the range. I've met a few cowboy bachelors, sourdoughs in their eighties and nineties, but most cowhands sowed their wild oats and then settled down to a wife and kids. Many hands married late. One old hand compared his kind to a legendary Montana wolf who outwitted veteran trappers and was finally taken by the scent of a she-wolf in a trap.

Mary Goodbar was seventeen when she married thirty-nine-year-old Clarence Graves, a bachelor cowboy who had already retired from the range to his own small spread. A neighbor to the Goodbars (he lived only seven miles away), Clarence had met the train when Mary and her family moved from Indiana to a homestead near Havre in north-central Montana. That was in 1911, when Mary was twelve.

"'Course he didn't decide he was gonna have me for a wife then, and I didn't decide I was gonna have him for a husband. To me, he was an ugly man, a great big guy, he was tall and weighed two hundred pounds and had red whiskers. Big for a cowboy, you say? He wasn't a cowboy anymore, he was just working on a ranch, like all cowboys did eventually."

Joe Hughes said a problem with the men in cow camps was their close-mouthed policy. "They didn't admit to things that bothered them, you never knew how a fella felt. Might be like me and write it down in a poem, but you never admitted to that either." Pearl, a tiny woman with loving eyes, changed all that for Joe, as Mary did for Clarence.

Mary said a favorite pastime for the newlyweds, a habit they kept up thoughout their marriage, was "settin' around the kitchen table to see who could talk the longest."

The table, covered with brightly colored oilcloth, was one of the few pieces of furniture in what the newlyweds called their "homestead shack." Mary said couples didn't take wedding trips in those days, "we just up and settled down in the house we intended to live in."

Mary described that home: "...one room, built sturdy, and two windows and a door. We had a kitchen range, table, some chairs and a bed covered with a spread made of bright-colored pieces left over from dresses and aprons. There were shelves on the wall, with canned milk and canned vegetables, some spices and a box of matches. On top of the warming oven on the stove was a can of salt and some pepper. Some pans hung behind the stove and a box nailed to the wall nearby held the dishes."

Of course Mary didn't know how to use all those cooking staples and pots and pans. She was raised by a hard-working mother and a 232-pound easy-going father who lived to be ninety-one and who, Mary said, "Could play a tune on a jug if he had a mind to." Mary could dance a jig and play a banjo, but she couldn't cook.

When Clarence asked for Mary's hand in marriage, her mother was scandalized—"What? A man older than your father?"—and her father exclaimed to Clarence "Why? She can't cook, she can't even boil water!"

"I'll teach her," Clarence replied.

Bachelor cowboys knew how to cook, and teaching Mary required a cowboy's patience. The first thing she did was mix up batter for a huge chocolate cake to take to a schoolhouse party. It didn't rise and was so heavy she could barely dump it out of the pan. Clarence took one look, laughed, and dumped it into the swill pail. "It went ker-plunk and sunk quickly to the bottom. The pigs liked it, I think, but I sure shed tears over it. Later I made some very nice cakes, but I always thought of the ker-plunk of that first one."

Next, Mary tried bread. When it didn't rise, she took it behind the barn, dug a hole in the dry manure pile and hastily buried the dough.

"I guess you know what happened. Clarence came home about dark, went around to the back of the barn to put the milk cow in, and stepped in that glob of goo clear up to his shoe tops. It scared him some because he had no idea what it was. It was dark and when he took the next step it went right along with him. It had been hot that afternoon and that stuff had more than risen in that manure. He lit the lantern in the barn and examined the white blob. Then he knew what it was."

Mary recalls that she was all prettied up, waiting for Clarence to come in for supper. He didn't say a word but took down his other pair of overalls. "I looked down at the pair he had on. He'd scraped off as much dough as he could but a lot was hanging on for dear life."

Mary said he looked pretty grim, but later he rolled on the bed and laughed until tears came to his eyes.

I first met this lively woman along the Bitterroot River in the 1970s. I can still see her and a gray-haired lady friend, dressed in denim coveralls, laughing as they ducked through brushy willows with their fishing poles. Twice-widowed and in her seventies, Mary said, "To grow old does not mean to stop." She pursued angling, guitar playing, painting and dancing into her eighties, and wrote accounts of early-day homesteading for a local paper.

"I write the way I talk. I guess I write by ear, just the way I play guitar, and cook, too," she laughed. She did become an excellent cook and was famous for her yeast rolls.

"Don't write a book about the way cowboying really was," Mary said as she put a cup of coffee and a plate of shortbread cookies at my elbow in her Hamilton home. "Most people think of the cowboy era as a romantic time, and they don't want to hear any different."

Mary grinned, "Let me tell you what they did on Sundays." A hand like Clarence, who worked year-round, got Sundays off when not on trail.

"Saturday night was for spiffin' up and going to a schoolhouse dance, so the men slept in Sunday morning. It was a day for staying near the bunkhouse. The major project was washing clothes," Mary said.

Washing heavy clothing encrusted with horse sweat was no easy job. Water had to be heated over the woodstove and poured into a metal tub or basin. Cowboy ingenuity led to the creation of a special clothes-washing device. The nearest Mary could come to labeling it was that it resembled a "toilet stomper."

"It was made first out of a small can with a piece of old tree or something stuck down in it, then a big old bucket was attached around the outer ring of the thing, so when you plunged it down there in your soapy water, those two cans would make quite a suds."

Mary said cowhands had quite a few clothes to wash, most of which were "overalls." The cowhand took up Levi's early, but he called them overalls, not jeans. Clarence had worked in northern Montana country known for fierce winters. "In the wintertime, now that was a job to wash their sourdoughs—they were canvas pants with blanket lining—they were the heaviest things. They didn't wash 'em often, by spring they stood alone."

On Sundays, a cowhand polished his boots with neat's-foot oil, patched and polished harnesses and other horse tack and replaced lost buttons. "Usually the lady of the ranch would give them some old buttons, and they'd sew 'em on no matter what the color," Mary said. She said she never saw a man wear a belt on a ranch in those days. "They wore suspenders, big wide ones. If they dressed up, like they usually did Saturday nights, they wore belts."

Clarence kept up his handy ways after the marriage. A gentle, good-natured giant, he pitched in with house chores. The picture Mary and Clarence bring to mind in their lantern-lit cabin is one that painter Charlie Russell sketched after his marriage. It showed an aproned Charlie merrily wiping the dishes as his bride washed.

"I lucked out, he was a wonderful man who showed me lots of love and respect," Mary said.

Nothing in Clarence's background suggested that he would grow up to be a model husband and father, but this is true of many old hands. In fact, Clarence's background has a familiar ring to it. His father left his mother and, after one too many beatings from the folks who were raising him, Clarence ran away from Indiana to become a cowboy in Montana. He was thirteen. He rode the rails and did odd jobs, making it to Chinook, south of the Canadian line in central Montana, by age fourteen. He found a cowboy job in the Bears Paw mountains of north-central Montana.

Unlike most cowboys, Clarence stayed at the same ranch a long time. One of the hands he worked with was Shorty Phillips. Shorty traveled from job to job but he and Clarence kept in touch. "He brought a sheep for a wedding gift and stayed three days," Mary laughed.

"I think we got married on a Wednesday," Mary explained, "and on Thursday along came old Shorty Phillips and he had a team and a buggy, a spring wagon, and he had a beautiful sheep in there. He said, 'You got room for my horse, don't you?' and we said, 'Oh, sure we got room for your horse.' 'Course we didn't have room for Shorty. Didn't matter, he stayed three days. I'll never forget that, he brought a wedding present and he stayed three days."

Mary and Clarence shared the same sense of humor, a gift that saw them through events a lot tougher than Shorty's visit. Homesteading a small ranch on Montana's "hi-line" (between the forty-eighth and forty-ninth parallels) brought battles against hail, grasshoppers, fires and floods. One of the worst calamities for the Graves family occurred when hail the size of golf balls came out of the blue one August day and killed everything—chickens, turkeys, crops. "We sure felt bad, so I took the cream I was gonna sell in town that day and we used the hailstones to make ice cream. Then we all felt better."

And there were those nightly talks around the kitchen table. Five kids—the first ones born one, two, three in the homestead shack, were tucked in bed with their harmonicas and the talks continued.

The story they laughed over the most was one Clarence told on himself.

It always annoyed him that modern men (men in the 1920s and 1930s) didn't even tip their hats to women, but he agreed he went a bit overboard.

"It was back in his cowboy days," Mary began, "and there was a schoolmarm teaching at one of those out-of-the-way schoolhouses. He was riding after some strays and he came across an old barbwire fence and he let the wire down and went across. Then he had to answer the call of nature so he let down his galluses [suspenders] and set down beside a sagebrush there. Now he always thought the schoolmarm went thataway, but she was on her saddle horse and went thisaway, come right up on top of him. He told me, 'I'll never forget that if I live to be a thousand. I jumped up, tipped my hat and grabbed my pants at the same time'."

Mary paused to wipe tears of laughter from her eyes. "He'd say to me, 'Why did I tip my hat to that poor woman? Her face was beet red and she was going like forty miles an hour.' We laughed over that so many times."

Of course it wasn't all laughter. Running your own place meant being self-sufficient and spending days alone while your man was out tending stock or hay fields or working odd jobs to eke out a living. "I used to stand by the kitchen window and look way off and see a sheepherder." Mary said, "He was a living person and I'd just stare at him because it had been days since I saw anybody."

Self-doctoring was another necessity in the wide-open West. Mary set aside a pantry shelf for cure-alls that had nothing in common with today's medicine cabinet. "I don't recall seeing a pill of any kind, but I think the same stuff's been mixed up and put in bottles and pills today. Our pantry shelf had cans of goose grease, skunk oil, turpentine, kerosene, lard, castor oil, salts, mustard, vinegar, flax seed and a shoe box full of nice clean woolen pieces from old underwear. 'Course there was a bottle of liquor for snake bites, and safety pins to pin on poultices."

Mary said having kids was a major diversion. "That's all you could do in those days, there wasn't any movies to go to or anything. I had the children all at home, but I never had 'em without doctors. You'd think our first was the first kid ever born, Clarence was so proud. He yelled all the way [half a mile] to my uncle's house, hollerin' the news that his son was born."

Clarence involved himself in the raising of the children. Poor as he and Mary were, one day a week he stayed home and insisted that she take off. "I'd go for a long walk, or take the saddle horse. Happened that the place close enough to visit was the home of my future daughter-in-law. Her parents lived on a ranch down by the creek. The wife had two little kids at that time and my daughter-in-law was one of them."

I told Mary that many contemporary fathers were trying to do what Clarence did well over a half-century ago, and she replied, "It sure did a good job for me. I could take care of them a lot better when I got home."

Clarence loved to sing. He sang to the kids all the time, and he'd tell them cowboy stories. Mary didn't know any stories that would interest the kids as much as cowboy escapades, so she made a movie house.

"I'd gone to the movies back in Indiana. The kids didn't know what movies were, never heard of 'em. Clarence was holding all three of the kids on his lap. There was an empty panel on the bedroom door, someone had broken in while we were gone one winter, and I set a lamp behind it and put a sheet over that panel and I cut out cowboys and horses and paper dolls, some dancing, and teams and sleighs—things like that—and led 'em across in front of that light. I recently asked Bob, my oldest boy—he's sixty-seven— if he remembered that, he said, 'Yes, Mom, I do'."

The children were grown and married by the time Mary nursed Clarence, ill with cancer. "He kept his good humor 'til the last, but then, he knew about dying, and about nursing. Cowboys took care of each other, that included the old ones who didn't have any place to go. My husband had to take care of an old boss he had—I don't know what he was dying from, but he was dying. Clarence stayed with him until he died. Aside from all his regular work, Clarence nursed him. The old man told him to get into a trunk he had and get his Bible and his rosary—[Clarence] never knew 'til then that the old man was Catholic. He wanted a priest. They had to send to Chinook and get one, he got there in time. That priest's name stayed with me, Ebensweiler...So my husband stayed with the old man until he died. That was his work, cowboys did everything. They didn't talk much about it, but they took care of themselves and most of the time each other so there wasn't anything they didn't do."

A good way to get the real scoop on any old hand is by talking to his wife.

Kenny and Verna Trowbridge in 1984. Photo by Jo Rainbolt

Kenny Trowbridge was a great talker, but Verna did all the phone-talking when I first met them. She said cowboys did not talk on the phone or go for the mail, and that they tended to leave the driving up to the wife. She also expressed the desire to get Kenny off the ground. She loved to fly and he had no interest.

All this changed after Kenny, a natural storyteller with Will Roger's wit and openness, became a fixture on the national folk festival circuit. He had to talk on the phone because of the arrangements involved. Verna would call, "Hello, Jo, he wants to talk to you." Kenny would holler and sputter into the phone, "*Jesus,* I got this goldurned bunch a stuff in the mail today, cain't tell hind-end from..." And I would offer to drive the few miles over, to eat some of Verna's cinnamon rolls and decipher the forms. Notice that Kenny mentioned mail. To Verna's amazement, he was collecting the mail, even looking forward to walking the two blocks to Darby's post office.

I still recall the first day Kenny actually dialed the phone himself. Verna was out and he had to let me know that our dear friend Tony Grace was in the hospital. Tony survived that hospital visit, but Kenny kept using the phone. He began to keep in touch with punchers as far away as Hawaii, fellow hands he met in 1982 and 1983 while touring the country with a group of singing, storytelling cowpunchers.

Verna was amazed at her luck. The Trowbridges celebrated their fiftieth wedding anniversary on cowboy Karin Haleauah's ranch in Hawaii, and in the summer of 1986 visited a son in Alaska. They'd never stayed overnight at any of their seven kids' homes before.

Verna just smiled and said she used to believe you can't teach an old dog new tricks.

Old couples warm the heart. I've never met a sweeter couple than Joe and Pearl Hughes. Before they were married, they had a spot along a trail where they left notes to each other. This inspired Joe to write "The Rose Garden Post Office," a poem he kept tacked to the wall in all the places he lived after Pearl died. Joe wrote the final verse to this poem after their sixtieth anniversary.

Wild roses grew from the mountain side,
A trail ran through where we could ride.
Long gone are many years.
Within the roses there's a cleft
Where many lovers' notes were left,
With many hopes and fears.

The trail is no more, the roses gone.
Though nothing else remains,

The love of yore still lingers on,
With all its joys and pains.

These notes of mine and yours
That held so many fears,
Held a pledge of love that still endures
Well over sixty years.

Joe's mother Ellen was probably his greatest influence. An Irish lass with pink cheeks, black hair and unusual perseverance, she came from County Cork, and worked as a housemaid for wealthy eastern families before meeting Joe's dashing father, a gardener who came to the new country to manage the Montana gardens of copper magnate Marcus Daly. She married badly, according to Joe, who couldn't tolerate the way his father treated his mother. "He was a boozehound, she had six kids, rough necks, and never knew what running water was, never knew what an indoor bathroom was…"

The only time I saw Joe's Irish temper was over matters concerning liars and men abusing women. He called modern cowboys show-offs; he'd grumble about their gaudy useless hats and the fact they always left them on their heads. When my youngest daughter, Kristen, and I took Joe to breakfast to celebrate his ninetieth birthday, he looked over the Sunday-morning crowd and snorted, "Wish I had my rusty old six-shooter with me, I'd shoot their hats right off their heads."

It wasn't easy to get stories from Pearl, although Joe encouraged her. "You talk, Joe," she'd say, her gentle, loving eyes never left his face as he told another adventure. Pearl was born into a pioneering family in the Bitterroot Valley. Her perky mother was an early-day postal carrier who took a buggy or sleigh and delivered mail twice a week to remote areas.

When I once included a few of Pearl's stories for a newspaper feature on old-time Christmases, Joe was pleased. "Pearl just won't blow her own horn," he said as he flipped sourdough hotcakes for the three of us. "Nobody knows how special she is."

Pearl beamed at my reply: "You know, Joe, and that's all that matters to Pearl."

Frances and Callie Billings presented a different kind of love story. Frances was a feisty and outspoken woman and Callie was quiet. She was forty-two when they married and he was fifty-three, a cowboy turned railroad worker. They had thirty good years before Callie died.

"We both liked the same things," Frances said, "that helps a marriage. We liked dancing, picnicking, hiking, all those silly things that young people do."

Both had had unhappy first marriages. "A lot of cowboys married, or at least courted, schoolteachers. Callie married one and she tried to make a bigshot out of him; can you imagine anyone making anything out of Callie that he wasn't?"

Frances married a would-be cowboy the first time around. "He pretended to be a cowboy. He didn't have a cowboy's standards. For one thing, he was tight. He'd set up the bar [drinks all around], but he wouldn't provide for his wife."

She recalled going into the saloon after one pay day and scooping the money right from the bar into her dress pocket. He didn't even notice her and when he did turn around, he said, "What are you doing, following me around like a goose?"

Frances left with full pockets. "That's why I still wear dresses with big pockets," she told me, chuckling.

Frances finally got out of her unhappy marriage. "I was divorced and had to have a job and all I could do was cook, so I started cooking out of a railroad car for crews. I met Callie in the cook car. I thought he was funny looking at first, I told him that afterwards. I didn't like men very well, I was badly abused the first time. He never struck me; I'd have killed him if he had...I was trying to hate all men, that's why I thought Callie was funny looking—it was the only thing I could think of. It wasn't easy to find anything wrong with him."

Callie and Francis

Joe and Pearl Hughes in 1980.
Photo by Jo Rainbolt

knew each other five months before they married. "We'd take long walks. We were in Logan, Montana, and walked six or eight miles to [the nearby town of] Manhattan. It was a Sunday and I didn't have to cook. We thought we'd eat dinner, but everything was closed except the bar. We couldn't get a meal until we got back to the beanery in Logan. I was used to walking and so was he. What did we do in our courtship besides walk? We went dancing, and he helped with the dishes in the cook car."

Frances smiled at the memory of Callie. "Callie always helped. Most men don't realize how much that means to a woman. Whenever I washed dishes, he wiped them. Now I just put them in the rack to dry. After he retired he always got breakfast, fixed my plate, saw to it that I ate it. I don't care much about breakfast. Oh, he was something. He had a keen sense of humor and he was always kind. He was never bossy but I knew where I stood with him. I knew I couldn't do a lot of things that a lot of women do, like nag."

The afternoon I interviewed Frances was shortly after her eightieth birthday, and she was annoyed that a saleswoman who had promised to drop in at eleven o'clock had never showed up. "It gets me, the way people promise things today and don't do it. Cowboys placed a premium on being honest, keeping your word. I don't like for people to tell me things if they're not going to do them."

Callie seldom got angry. One time he bawled Frances out for buying some used furniture. When he finished, she said, "Have you said all you're going to say?" and when he replied yes, she said, "I didn't hear a word you said."

Callie laughed, and he never bawled Frances out again for spending money. "I never did overspend. See that glass display case in the corner? That was a piece of furniture I bought that day, it cost a few dollars and it's so valuable now I've written it into my will."

I always enjoyed visiting Callie and Frances in their bungalow. I remember him as a typical old hand, a gentle, good-natured man who made good strong coffee and wore his felt cowboy hat and Pendleton plaid shirt to the last. A reluctant story-teller, he one day told me a story from his cowboy past. He was barely a boy, herding cattle in western Montana, camped out in a canvas lean-to, when he was visited by a friendly stranger wearing a colorful sash. Of course he asked the stranger to stay for supper. Only later did he find out that it was artist Charlie Russell, roaming the country, looking for landscapes and faces to paint and draw.

Frances said she never thought of remarrying after Callie died, even though she was in her prime, only seventy-two. "Never know what you're getting in for. And nobody could replace Callie. Old cowboys are special, and so are old railroad men. He was both. I heard a lady who had been a nurse say that the best patients, the kindest and most even-tempered, the best ones to get along with, were the cowboys and railroad men."

"And they made the best husbands, too, if the old hands I know are any example," I added.

"You bet," Frances replied.

All this changed in modern times. The code got fuzzy. Cowboys were still romantic, but word was out that they treated their horses better than their women. Whether this is true I cannot say. I have yet to marry a cowboy, although it didn't work when I tried a gentleman rancher. I do know quite a few cowboys and they are perplexed. Their ex-wives appear to take unfair advantage through the court system. One cowboy acquaintance was forced to pay his teenaged stepson $35,000 for ranch labor after he'd raised the boy. Another left the ranch to his ex-wife so the kids could grow up on it, even though she had divorced him for another man. Still another lost his ranch to his third wife. He claimed they were married only two months. When asked, "Why don't you cowboys fight back? Why let your women take such advantage?" he replied, "Chivalry—and it's almost dead."

***If you didn't have a horse's butt for a compass
you'd be a lost boy.***

Kenny Trowbridge's father to Kenny

From Tony Grace's collection, an electri- fying moment for Soapy Williams on Cox.

From the Bunkhouse
to the Outhouse

"Old Nig" was such an impressive horse he was twice rustled from his owner, Bill Chaney, and sold to unsuspecting buyers. Both time Bill found his big black horse, described distinctive marking under the horse's foreleg, and was able to buy Old Nig back. The horse came into Montana Territory in 1864. Bill raised him somewhere in the Midwest and, of course, he came along when Bill became wagonmaster for one of the first expeditions into the area that is now Montana.

Cowboy-artist J.K. Ralston liked to tell stories about Old Nig. He even painted the horse's most spectacular feat, calling his work "The Fate of the Mail Carrier."

The incident happened in eastern Montana during the days when there were more U.S. Army forts than towns. Nig's owner and another fellow were leaving Fort Buford for Fort Keogh, a trek of about a hundred miles. "They were both plainsmen, the colonel or whoever was in charge had an orderly flag 'em down, asked if they'd keep an eye out for a mail carrier who hadn't shown up," J.K explained.

Sixty-five miles along the way, they found the mail carrier's body amid scattered letters, in timber along the Yellowstone River. He'd been killed by Indians. While looking the situation over, Bill and his companion discovered they were being surrounded, and took off. They managed to keep ahead of their Indian pursuers, and swim the Yellowstone. Trouble was, Bill's partner's horse swam the river, then died on the opposite shore.

"Old Nig took both men the distance, right into Fort Keogh," J.K. finished with satisfaction.

Heroic-horse deeds are standard cowboy fare. What impressed me was J.K.'s story about Old Nig's funeral.

"That horse was over thirty-two when he died. Bill took up a ranch on the Yellowstone and kept Old Nig, carried him through the winters. They lose their teeth, so ya gotta feed 'em soft stuff, gruel and oats off the shelf. The hired man from the ranch was still living when I painted the picture. He's been right there in this house [J.K.'s home in Billings]; he told me this story.

"He was a young fella, about eighteen, and was working for Bill when the horse died. Bill told him to go up on the hill and dig a grave, so he went up there and dug a big hole. Then Bill told him to make a stone boat [sledge] to put [the horse] on. [Bill] said, 'We're not dragging him on the ground....' So they rolled him onto the stone boat and hauled him up on the hill, unloaded him and put him in there.

"Old Bill was sittin' up there on the side hill, after so long he said, 'Well, you'd better cover him up.' So the fellow started throwing dirt on him. Old Bill said, 'Wait a minute, don't shovel any more, don't shovel any direct in that horse's eyes. Nobody ever threw dirt in his eyes while he was living and we're not going to do it now.' So they covered his eyes and buried the horse. He's there today, on that ranch."

Cowboys indeed catered to their horses. Individuals made their favorites into pets, and most outfits didn't even give up on spoiled horses but kept them in a rough string.

Tony Grace described the attachment this way: A cowhand never walked when he could ride, from the saloon to the livery stable across the street, or from the bunkhouse to the outhouse.

"But why did you bother to keep rough horses when horses were a dime a dozen in Montana?" I asked Tony.

"Good question," he replied. "I never gave it any thought. I suppose it had something to do with hoping they'd improve."

I grinned. "You just couldn't give up on them."

Tony chuckled, "Yup, we were sentimental about 'em. And a lot of [rough horses] were above average—good strong horses, just ornery. It's hard to teach a horse after a certain age, they're like people in that respect. So the big outfits would pay a man extra to ride 'em. Some of these horses were too rough for the average cowboy. Some old cowboys, good cowboys in every sense of the word, wouldn't get on a bucking horse knowingly. Been on 'em, knew what a horse could do, just had no taste for it."

Tony got along well with horses; he could read them. And this was the boy whose only horse experience before he came west had been on a carousel. "Hard to explain, I just always knew I was gonna love working with horses, it was a strong feeling I had. I loved horses and I still do and I never did anything to deliberately hurt a horse."

Tony broke thousands of horses, his method being to figure out the horse and act accordingly. "Handling horses took a lot of patience, you study a horse and try to figure out his disposition. A stubborn horse is like a stubborn person, maybe you can handle him, maybe you can't. Horses are born different—some'll break real quick, real easy; others you can never teach, no matter how well they're handled. A lot of bucking horses are spoiled by early handling. I made a point of keeping my lessons short, on an average I wouldn't spend more than twenty minutes on a horse. Don't sour him, don't overdo it. Talk to the horse; they soon learn your voice and get acquainted."

Kenny Trowbridge said the same thing. "Ya can't learn a horse a goddam thing until ya got his attention. Same as people. Now, I'm talkin' about makin' somethin' of him, not one of these modern horses walkin' up and down the road with his head snappin' around. Horses knew somethin' back then, didn't just ride up and down the road. Once ya got a horse's attention, ya gotta be careful nuthin' spooks him, jes' like a kid—somethin' happens, they don't trust ya anymore."

Kenny said the best example of a horse breaker he came across was Tom Stucky, a black man from Montana's Big Hole Valley who claimed to be half Spaniard. "This one horse was an outlaw, damn thing wanted to eat ya. Stucky told the owners, 'For a sack a oats and twenty dollars, I'll break that horse.' I saw him do it. For two or three days he never went inside the damn corral, he talked to that damn horse. Got his confidence. In a week the rancher's wife was ridin' him up and down the lane. Stucky got his number, that horse never even bucked. Only two reasons a horse'll buck ya—he's scared or ya make him buck by sprurrin' him or eggin' him on.

"Ya git so you can size 'em up by lookin' at 'em. Bunch a horses, twenty-one head, I looked 'em over and finally said, 'I kin ride everyone of 'em but that brown.' The owner nodded, 'Ya called it goddam right, he's the only horse that ever throwed me'."

Tony, Kenny, and most of the old hands of my acquaintance opposed severity of any kind when dealing with horses. Kindness worked. "The thing was," Tony said, "you had to be kind to the horses…I'm speaking of normal horses—once in a while you got a knothead nuthin' would change much, but most horses responded to kindness."

Not all cowhands treated horses with a gentle touch. Quirts were standard equipment for cowhands of the 1880s and 1890s, and still were common in Tony and Kenny's day. Long winter months between roundups meant time for working with rawhide, and rawhide meant quirts. "Quirts were common," Tony said. "Good thing they were eliminated, they were abandoned completely. A guy would get mad and he'd draw a quirt and hit a horse. They were severe because the handle usually had a weight in it, and the popper on the end usually had two strips of rawhide, pretty stiff stuff to lay across a horse's flank, which is where they'd hit lots of times."

And, of course, not all cowhands exercised kindness and patience while breaking horses. Breaking meant breaking, and so what if a horse's spirit went along with it? Joe Hughes got so angry when a hand put a gunny sack over a horse's head he took up the challenge to break the animal himself, and injured his neck when it threw him headfirst into a post.

"Wild Horse" Wes Wright, in 1980, with a favorite horse, Victor. Photo by Jo Rainbolt

Tony came across the blind method of horse breaking while breaking mustangs for the KM outfit in Arizona. "They had these sixty head, run 'em right into the corral, none of them had been roped. No, I'll take that back, they may have been branded when they were first caught. I have an idea they were branded, but they were just as wild after roping and branding. If anything, wilder—roping and branding wouldn't have tamed 'em any. The foreman said, 'Tell me how many you want tied up' and I said 'I'll take four head.' So he dropped a loop on one, we rassled around with it, got a hackamore on it, fifteen feet o' rope on it and run it into a separate corral and turned it loose."

Four horses were roped and ready, the remaining put to pasture. Tony was told to get his saddle, and one mustang was roped and dragged into the now-empty big corral. "The foreman asked me to use a blindfold, a hackamore with a leather bandage you could slip up and down. I had never used this blind method, it was the Mexican style...I got my saddle on this pony, 'course he bucked like hell, being saddled without halter-breaking him. Rassled him around and got him saddled, pulled the blind down. I didn't like it. See you blind 'em and turn 'em loose and they hit the fence once or twice and that takes the buck out of 'em. They know they better stay put 'til that blind is up, so you can get aboard and then you reach over and pull that blind up, and then of course they'll move, they might buck and they might not."

Tony got the four horses bucked out without getting thrown but he decided to do the rest his own way. "My way was to first halter break 'em, handle and gentle them a little bit. I saddled 'em, unsaddled 'em, did all sortsa things to prepare them."

Before Tony worked on those other fifty-four mustangs, he got "jobbed" on a fifth horse. "Jobbing meant tricking," Tony explained, and went on to tell how he was jobbed. "The boss said, 'Tony I've got a horse in that corral been handled some but never been rode, he needs breaking.' So after I had my dinner I walked down and I looked that horse over and his tail had been pulled and he looked like a horse that had been around. Ha. Anyway, I knew I was being jobbed. I didn't know the history of that horse, I learned that later."

Tony knew he was going to get bucked and was prepared for it. He took a short hold on his braided cotton rope rein. The horse pulled his head down and took Tony with him. "Stood me right square on my head, I had a good grip on that rein, it was unraveled so my hold would stay, and I couldn't run my fingers through it soon enough."

But believing "not a horse that can't be rode...," Tony decided this was a horse he could ride. The next morning he went to the shop and adjusted his spurs so the rowel would lock. "If I grabbed the horse with my spurs they'd go far enough in so they wouldn't revolve. This helps you stay on the horse, like a coupla hooks. They weren't doing the horse any damage, maybe took a little hair off. I went to the corral and saddled Mister Horse and rode him to a standstill. Come to find out he was a horse been used in a contest in Williams, Arizona—fella named Jim Schmidt won first money on him. Ended up they sold that horse, he ended up in the Prescott rodeo bareback string. So I can say I rode one contest horse and completed the ride."

New hands often were jobbed, handed a horse by a foreman saying, "Here, this one's real gentle." It was all in good-natured fun, but horse-play went further than that. Mean-spirited cayuses sometimes were used as pawns in a cowboy game between two men who couldn't get along, as was the case with the most natural bronc rider Tony came across in his six-state, sixty-year career. Smokey Moore, one of Teddy Roosevelt's rough riders in Cuba was the man, and Smokey knew he was good.

"He was fifty-three years old when he was with me in Seligman, Arizona," Tony recalled. "He didn't hit it off with the boss, they clashed right from the first. Smokey wasn't the easiest guy to get along with, but he was a bronc rider. Smokey and the foreman were clashing every day or so, there wasn't much done about it, but I knew something was gonna break soon. The foreman was a little bit of a man, he really wasn't a man you cared much for. He didn't have much personality. I guess he knew his business, up to a point."

Smokey rode every horse in the remuda, and "made monkeys out of all of 'em," Tony said. The ranch owned two outlaws famous in the area, horses too ornery for the regular string. Mountain Gray was the toughest, and the hands kept speculating over what would happen when the foreman put the gray horse in the remuda. Obviously, the mean bird would go to old Smokey. Some men bet on Smokey, some on Mountain Gray.

"Mountain Gray was a well-put-together gray horse, muscular, a little bit on the chunky side yet not overly chunky, had lot of flexibility, a lot of action. On that outfit the foreman did catch the saddle horses each morning; on a lot of outfits I rode with ya roped your own. So, one morning the foreman brought in Mountain Gray and asked Smokey to bring his saddle over. Smokey was wearing a little city hat—he did have on boots, no chaps. He got his saddle on, I knew something was gonna happen but I didn't realize how much would happen. Smokey got in that left stirrup and when he swung his right leg over instead of fishing for that right stirrup he just fished for that right shoulder and hit him with that spur. 'Course the gray really exploded— for a little horse he did a real good job. It wasn't a rodeo arena, it was on fairly rough ground. Smokey really worked him over. He spurred him forward and back. It sure tamed down the opposition."

Did Mountain Gray become a kitten? No, but he became Smokey's favorite horse. "Smokey liked the horse. As often was the case among outlaws, they were good. They were tough and they were good and they had a lot of staying power. And Smokey liked that.

"He used the gray to show up the foreman's favorite, a fellow by the name of Nick Peck. He and Smokey didn't get along one bit. Nick was after a cow and a yearling—I dunno just why, the yearling might have been unbranded, I dunno why they wanted to catch the cow. Anyway, Nick was swinging his rope, he was after that cow, and Smokey came along and built a loop and passed him and caught the cow and hogtied her. In the meantime Nick took after the yearling and Smokey built another loop and took after it and caught it, too, riding that outlaw. He was a character."

Tony dug up a photo of himself with a group of Arizona hands, including Smokey Moore. The latter was a tanned, good-looking man, squatting in the dust in white shirt and tweeds, wearing a dress hat (what Tony called a "city hat"), and an ironic grin.

Tony peered at the photo, "Yup, a character. One time he and another top bronc man rode an outlaw horse double...and they stayed aboard. I was there but I didn't see it, wish I had. This photo was taken before Smokey went back to Miles City. He was on his way to Niagara Falls to where his wife was, going after her, and he stopped in Miles City and won first money on the regular roundup [the hands' own bucking contest after the roundup]."

Who can explain horse rapport? "Wild Horse" Wes Wright grew up on a sheep ranch his father started near Malta on Montana's hi-line in the late 1880s. "I growed up half-horse, I liked to horse race, ride buckin' stock. All that was strictly agin my father's religion and he tried to beat it outa me."

Wes, when he was nearly eighty, lived alone in a tin trailer with enough acreage to support his extended family of horses, including huge Belgian work horses. Too stove up from horseback injuries to ride, he led teams and even did his haying with horses. Feeding time could be dangerous to a camera-toting onlooker. "Kerful, now," he hollered at me over his shoulder as a dozen horses cavorted up, "they dunno how big they are."

Wes liked to train range horses, the kind Tony was referring to when he said they were like putting bull elk into a corral. Wes explained, "I liked to take a young horse, the wilder they were the better I liked 'em—the easier they were to handle. Used to be horses weren't all gentle and halter broke like nowadays."

Wes learned his methods from an old Indian man who worked for his dad. "He was a good horse hand, a whale of a good hand: Alec Parrant. He showed me a lot, and I remembered it, how to neck rope 'em and front-foot 'em."

I asked Wes if his method for breaking horses was common. "Well, it was for me. That's the way I done it," he replied.

After roping a horse by the front feet and getting him down, Wes put the hackamore on. "We always kept a picket log around, put 'em on one of them picket logs before they was halter broke. After they'd been on that picket, I could just untie the rope and they'd lead right off. I got a big old flat wheel I use out here, not a log. They can drag it—I never tied 'em to anything solid, always tied 'em to something [that] if they run on it, they could move it. That was their first lesson. Then I'd halter break 'em, get 'em used to a rope on the ground."

Wes never met a horse he couldn't break, and he never broke a horse's spirit. "Everythin' gotta keep its spirit. My old man tried to git mine. Never could please him."

When Wes finally had enough of his dad's treatment, he got himself a green-broke bronc and got the kinks out of it on the two-day ride east to

Glasgow, Montana. He worked for the David and Nelson cow outfit until his dad coaxed him back home. "I stayed there 'til he finally killed himself, then I had to take over the ranch, since my mother knew nuthin' about it. By that time we was out of sheep and raising bulls."

Other ranch-born men, such as Tom Harwood, were luckier with their fathers. Tom's easy-going Blackfeet Indian father was a bronc peeler. He rode rough-string for a number of Montana's big outfits, meaning he knew horses well enough to keep the feisty ones halfway controlled. The elder Harwood was hard to beat in the riding business, but he never talked horses.

Tom said, "Dad was kind of, I guess you'd call it close-mouthed. He never said too much. I've heard more from other people who knew Dad when he was young and rode horses with him than I ever heard from him."

Tom warmed to any subject, but he lighted up when he talked horses. "I didn't pretend to be no bronc twister, but I rode a lot of horses..." he began, and described how at age sixteen he became "horse king" of the Cut Bank area, on the east side of the present boundaries of the Blackfeet Indian Reservation.

It all took place in the late 1910s. Homesteaders were moving into northern Montana, raising cattle and crops, chickens and sheep and horses on their 160-acre spreads. A drought year came, the homesteaders ran out of grass, and Tom's parents took in stock to pasture. "The homesteaders didn't have money to pay their pasture bill, and just kept leavin' [the animals]. Finally the folks moved down to this place [where Tom and his wife Ruby lived, south of the previous ranch and near Valier]. We had all this watered land, forty-four hundred acres in that one field was our land. 'Course at that time all this was [Blackfeet] reservation.

"All the guys who had stock told me to make a circle, told me to take their stock, they didn't wanna fool with 'em. I just took 'em, put my brand on 'em and turned 'em out, cattle and horses. Guys that raised horses to sell got me to round 'em up and I got to keep the suckers and yearlings. I was kinda the horse king of the country. I was just a kid then, about sixteen. I had more horses than I knew what to do with. I'm that way yet, I guess. We got about thirty or forty head o' horses up there on the ridge now."

Old hands might forget men's names, but they have uncanny recall where horses are concerned. I asked Tom if any horses stood out from the hundreds he has owned.

"Favorites? Oh yes, I've had a lot of favorites. I had a little bay horse that was an awful good little horse. I raised him. I call him Thirty-One. He was born on the thirty-first of May, lived to be thirty-one, and died on the thirty-first of May. God, he was a good one—fast."

"I had a pinto horse one time, a black and white, a very beautiful horse—a big horse, too, had size on him. I had him a long time. Got a little age on him, an outfit came in, wanted him, they had more money than they had sense and offered me an awful price so I just took it. The old horse was ready to lay down any time. Then I hadda sorrel mare...made a pack horse outa her first, but she turned out to be kinda gentle so we just kinda wrangled with her, one thing or another. But every colt she had was a good one. Boy, she raised some good colts."

Donovan McGee knew some horses that couldn't be called good ones, but he liked them just the same. Don adhered to the philosophy of all old horse breakers: it's necessary to like a horse and respect his personality in order to train him. And it must be kept in mind that all horses will not do all things. This was the case with three of Don's favorites—Dumb Head, Angel, and Bones.

Don was only fifteen when he took on Dumb Head, a horse that had to be "four-footed" (hobbled) and blindfolded in order to saddle, but was indispensable for rounding up wild range horses. "No way you could work cattle with him, but you could sure run horses. That Dumb Head could run fifteen to twenty miles and never slow down. Trouble is, you couldn't stop him. One time nature called and I couldn't get off, had to wet my pants."

Angel was a pretty little dark bay. He'd kick, strike and bite until Don was safely in the saddle, then he'd run all day. "You'd get off and on with care, but you could do it," Don said.

Bones was a big old rawboned horse. "To all appearances he was a plow-horse, but he could run like a streak of lightning. You couldn't ride him if he didn't take a notion to let you."

Having settled in Alaska after World War II and traded his saddle for a trolling boat, Don said simply, "I miss horses very much."

Early in the 20th century, cowboys still trained horses for the military. Not just for American armed forces, but also for the armies of England, France and Italy.

Tony found that a good place to winter over when jobs were scarce was Fort Keogh in Miles City. A military fort when the U.S. Army fought the Indians, it by then had become a remount station, supplying broken horses for cavalry and artillery forces.

"There were five breaking barns," Tony explained. "I was in Barn One, the cavalry barn, and the next barn to us was the artillery barn. We took green horses and broke 'em to ride and they went to what they called the gentle barn, a finishing deal. They paid us cowboy wages, forty dollars a month. We worked only so many hours, none of this three and four o'clock breakfasts like you had on the spring roundup. The nice thing about it was you didn't have to rush yourself, could take all the time you needed. I really learned a lot about breaking horses."

Tony traveled by train from his horse-breaking work in Miles City to Chicago, to show horses to French, Italian and English buyers. "They were buying war horses. I worked in the French inspection. We lined the horses up, saddled them, walked and trotted them down, then ran them back so the buyers could test their wind." Tony said he and a partner he recalled as Brownie rode 110 horses in a single day, but he believed Bob Finley and *his* partner held the record with 130.

Art Wahl in his 70s . Portrait by Lee Nye, courtesy
of Astrid Wahl Batchelder

"The English bought the best horses and paid the most money, the French were next in line in that respect, then the Italians—they paid the least and got the poorest horses. Wages [in Chicago] were ten dollars a day, which was very, very big money for forty-dollar-a-month hands to be drawing. However, out of that we paid our own room. which in those day didn't amount to much. We stayed in roominghouses. Was it fun? Sure. Men from Wyoming, Nevada, Oklahoma, Colorado..."

Tony and Art Wahl were both drafted during World War I, but they saw a different kind of action than did most servicemen. As with many cowboys, their assignment was to break horses in Fort Lewis, Washington. Tony said, "We rode a lot of horses daily but it was more of an exercise deal, a gentling deal. They were horses that had already been started. We had miles and miles of country to ride in."

It was common for a cowboy to break a rancher's horses in exchange for a horse of his own. When teenaged Joe Hughes was ready to move on from his job for Mark Real Bird on the Crow Reservation, Real Bird offered him a trade. If Joe broke two horses for the ranch, he could keep a horse for himself. Always diligent, Joe spent a month saddle-breaking the two and picked out a green horse to keep. Riding a horse into a river— in this case, the Bighorn— was a common way to get the bucks out. Trouble was, Joe's horse drowned.

Art Wahl was serving at Fort Lewis, Washington, breaking cavalry horses, when he and his older brother, Knute, posed together in uniform. Courtesy of Astrid Wahl Batchelder

"When I left, the women gave me some moccasins. I guess they figured I'd be walking for a while," Joe said.

Joe was no stranger to walking. Starting at age seven, he'd hop onto anything that moved, and when you do that you get bucked off occasionally and walk back to the ranch. A poem on that very subject tickled Joe so much he could barely repeat the last stanza:

> *It looks like I'm due for one hell of a spill.*
> *I roped a wild horse while we're going downhill.*
> *There's two other horses run into my rope,*
> *I'm tied hard and fast and there isn't much hope.*
> *I just about figured that I'd better quit,*
> *And when it's all over, I'll find where I lit.*

"That's just about it. Shows him about ready to quit his horse," Joe chuckled. "He had all these horses tangled up in his rope, ya know."

Such things happened when you ran wild horses, especially when you tied hard and fast (tied the rope to the saddle horn). Joe said he always tied hard and fast, because he'd seen too many cowhands who lost fingers while dallying a rope, or paying it out by hand.

After he left Real Bird, young Joe's next job was riding for a German rancher named Anner who ran stock in the Bighorn country of southeastern Montana. There he heard about a legendary wild mare running in the area around Fort Custer.

"She was tough, about fourteen, fifteen years old, and been runnin' in those hills. She used to be at the lead of a band of more or less half-wild horses. She was a mare, can you imagine her running in the lead? Different ones tried to get her, corral her, but she'd never been corraled."

"She was old, why'd they want to break her?" I asked.

"Why does anybody want to break a horse? Because she was the toughest and fastest thing there on that range. If you wanted something to run wild horses with, she was it. I had that in mind some."

Joe wanted the mare, and when he heard she'd been corraled, he traded her from the fellow who caught her. I overlooked asking him what he traded, probably everything he had (except the Indian moccasins, which he kept all his life).

"After I got ahold of her, I thought 'She'll be a tough one to handle,' and she *was* tough. I tamed her by riding her. Pulled a bit in two one time on her. She was a pretty good size, bigger than your average cayuse I guess, kind of a ginger color. I called her Ginger. She was pretty well built. I still have scars where the barb wire got in the way, she tore up my leg in a barb wire fence. You had a lot of accidents on that horse, and she was only one."

Joe's worst accident on Ginger kept him lying down "with a cracked leg" in a small, dim, isolated granary for six weeks. "The granary was the only place had a cover on it.

"It was a kick—you couldn't say I was throwed off, I jumped off. She jumped a cut one day, it was a deep cut [gully] and she caught her front feet and was hangin' there, a-fallin' and a-scramblin' and I seen the bank. I jumped off and went down and she caught the bank and got up before I could get up. I hung onto the hackamore and she got me behind her and—whammo—she battered me. She jumped over me and kicked me with her feet.

"So I laid in that granary to heal—man, I had pain. Oh, man! Anner, he used to check on me, he'd soak my leg with hot baths, he'd studied medicine a little. He was a good fellow. It sure hurt. I still got a knot in there."

While Joe was laid up, a man who rounded up wild horses for a living stopped by the cow camp to take a look at Ginger. "His name was Joe Hinman. He woulda bought her if he could ride her. I was able to get up and get to the door of the granary just far enough so I could see him. He rode her, [but] he didn't take any chances—she was still bucking. He really had that horn with both hands, I knew he was having plenty of trouble staying on. We joked about it, 'Well, boys, if that horn doesn't pull out he's got her rode.' All the hands were watching. When he came back over to where I was in the granary, he said 'She's too wild, I don't think you'll ever get it out of her'."

"And did you?" I asked Joe Hughes.

"Oh, yes, I broke her. I wanted to take her back to the Bitterroot with me in the fall of 1913, but she got with colt. Imagine running all those years and she never had a colt. See, after I broke her and she was used to being handled, we got her in with Anners' horses and here she got with colt. I had to go and didn't want to make the trip with her while she was with colt, so I left her there, traded her off for town lots in Park City [southwest of Billings in central Montana]. I was a property owner—I wasn't of age but I was a property owner. I kept 'em about twenty years, then I traded 'em off for lots in California back when things were worth nuthin'."

Joe believed that water under the bridge is just that. Still, there was a feeling of nostalgia, a wistfulness, when he told me the story of the tough wild mare. Like Joe and Tony and all the old hands, she belonged to a different time.

People who aren't saddle broke...can wear the fancy Stetsons and cowboy boots but it still sticks out all over 'em that they're phonies.

Tony Grace

Dressed to kill—and mock the cowboy myth—in an Idaho photographer's studio, 1928, are (left to right): the Luke brothers, Kenny Trowbridge (age 17), and "Granny" Duchett. Author's collection

How the West Was Worn

The western clothing fad that swept the nation in the early 1980s didn't touch Montana. If anything, working cowboys became more conservative, going back to unadorned boots and low-crowned, moderate-brimmed hats rather than be mistaken for dudes. After I visited Milwaukee in the spring of 1981, I could hardly wait to tell Tony Grace.

"You should have seen the Minneapolis airport, businessmen in Stetsons and fancy boots. Same on the streets of Milwaukee. My city sister took me to lunch wearing hundred dollar cowboy boots. Even the waitresses wore cowboy stuff. The farther east you go, the more you see it..."

"Good," Tony replied. "I'd feel better about goin' back east now. I hate to put on a little dude hat and low-cut shoes. I don't wear them here, but I had to when I went back there [for his dude ranch business in the 1930s and 1940s] or I'd have people staring and even yellin' at me."

Tony chuckled, "It's so easy to spot people who aren't saddle broke; they can wear the fancy Stetsons and cowboy boots but it still sticks out all over 'em that they're phonies. They just don't handle themselves right."

An early cowhand handled himself right and, according to Tony, he needed only a few items of clothing to be dressed for the part. "Hat, shirt, boots and pants. But one thing about 'em, what they wore was the best."

A hat might be retired after years of hard use, but was often kept as a souvenir. "Hats? You interested in hats? I can show you my first felt..." and Tony ambled off in search of a seventy-five-year-old flat-brimmed Stetson he bought in Aberdeen, South Dakota, on his way west in 1911.

J.K. Ralston presented a capsule history of hats when asked if he had an old favorite. "I've got a Stetson that's unique, goes clear back to the time of the Civil War. Original old Stetson. Now it's not the very first, they had raw brims and this one has a bound brim. The first two styles are identical except for the brims."

J.K. talked of how hatmaker John B. Stetson came west in the 1860s for the same reason many easterners did. He was a sickly young man and embarked on an expedition to Pike's Peak, Colorado for his health. I don't know about health, but after settling back in Philadelphia, he did acquire wealth. He decided the westerners needed a broad-brimmed hat, and created one by pulverizing dried rabbit skins into felt. One of Stetson's most popular styles was the one J.K. had—"Boss of the Plains."

"It came in three sizes," J.K. said. "Small, middle and large. Most cowpunchers wore them middle-sized, but once in a while you might see a man with a big one and occasionally a small one. They had a high crown but not real high. You could get them either black or white. A lot of cowhands wore white, but plenty wore black, too. I had an uncle, an old-timer bronc rider, and he never wore anything but a black hat. I think it was his personal preference, he had black whiskers."

Joe Hughes found it amusing that grimy, sweat-rimed, beat-up hats have actually become collector's items. Joe still wore the same style he wore as a young hand, only he had switched from white to black. A familiar figure around Hamilton, Montana, Joe could be spotted blocks away by his large black beaver felt hat. No-nonsense Joe left the crown undented and the brim flat except for a slight "pencil curl" around the edge. "Same way I wore it for seventy years," Joe said. Joe's hat always looked clean and lint-free, as if he'd just finished brushing and blocking it.

Early hats came with a flat brim, which the storekeeper creased in the desired style, or the cowhand did it himself over a teakettle. Hands often poked a distinctive dent in top of their hats, then poked it out again when rain fell.

Kenny Trowbridge said there were only a few hat styles in the early 1900s and the brims were bigger, like Joe's. Unlike Joe, most hands turned up the front or sides of a hat. Kenny wore a well-used dark-brown felt turned up in a three-corner style that gave a triangular effect to the brim, a standard old-time style in western Montana and Idaho. J.K. Ralston wore a silver-grey short-brimmed hat with a pinched front crown reminiscent of Roy Rogers. Tony's short-brimmed hat was a typical rancher's style.

Kenny Trowbridge said you could tell which part of the country a cowhand came from by the style and color of his hat, since whole outfits tended to adopt one style. Marjorie Young, an elderly woman from Miles City, showed me an original copy of a handwritten trail song written by an anonymous cowhand from the old XS outfit. It begins, "We are the punchers from the Yellowstone Flats, who wear the high heels, also the white hats…"

The white hat Joe Hughes wore as a young man almost landed him in jail. Joe said two men had been seen stealing a good race horse from a barn near Hamilton. They got away, which wasn't too difficult in those days. "No phones, no automobiles—a guy could take off across the country with almost anything and not be apprehended."

Local law officers were on the lookout for a tall man and a short man, both wearing white hats. "The very next day, I and George Lucas rode—no, we drove into town. Had a team and a spring wagon. Lucas was about five-feet six [Joe was a stringy six-footer], and we fit the description perfectly."

Joe said he was amused when he and his friend were picked up by the deputy sheriff, Henry Gilmore. "It kinda tickled me. I knew he should know me. He used to ride with my brother, I went to school with his sister. But I'd been away since I was sixteen and I guess he didn't remember me. By the time we walked down to the jail, he said, 'I'm beginning to think you *are* a Hughes,' and he didn't take us in."

Joe continued to wear a white hat, but he wrote Joe Hughes around the brim of it.

White hats didn't stay white very long. Out of all the cowhand's gear, hats probably took the most beating. "A Stetson you could roll right up and stick in your bedroll, then bend it back into shape again," Joe said. "The hat made quite a weapon, it was a natural instinct to beat something with your hat. First thing you'd do is grab for your hat and hit a critter with it. You could fan a bronc, stop an angry cow. So hats didn't stay white very long."

Kenny Trowbridge said hats were even used for stakes in bets. "It was common to hear, 'Bet you a new hat.' Did they keep the bet? Goddam right they did."

A hand might buy another fellow a hat, but he'd never give his away. It was as personal as his saddle. A hat shielded the cowhand from the sun and worked as an umbrella during thunderstorms. A thirsty hand could drink from it, a sleepy hand could grab a few winks with his hat as a pillow. A hat was used as a fan around smoky campfires. A cowboy almost lost his identity without a hat.

Seventy-year-old Montana singer-cowboy Earsel "Swede" Bloxham had never flown before he was invited to a St. Louis folk festival, but his only question did not concern travel. It was summer, and he wondered if he should wear his straw or his felt. His wife Thelma settled it when she said firmly, "You'll wear your felt." Felt hats have individuality and style, especially Swede's, a low-crowned Gene Autry style.

Cowboys' boots reflected the fact that cowhands had an aversion to walking. The slanted heels were set back of the side seam of the boot, creating a strong shank for the stirrup but a weak shank for walking. Well-made modern boots, on the other hand, have the heel set ahead of the side seam, giving the boot a shorter, stronger shank. Modern cowboys can actually *walk* from the bunkhouse to the outhouse.

Just as old-timers talk about "real hands," they mention "real boots." A real boot had a high heel well set under, a strong shank and a well-shaped foot. Boot leather was generally French calf, morocco or kid. Hands didn't think twice about spending a month's wages for boots. "We didn't have much, what we had was quality," Tony said.

Hands took pride not only in good boots but also in small feet. A small boot slipped easily out of the stirrup and looked pretty, too. It was an insult to call a man a "clodhopper," meaning he had big feet like a farmer, a walker. Silk socks often were necessary under the sleek-fitting boots. Kenny said some hands went so far as to order boots a size and a half smaller than shoes.

"People have bigger feet nowadays, running barefoot or in low-heeled shoes, allowing feet to spread," Tony said. He wore a size six in his riding days.

"Not many ready-made boots back then," Tony said. "Most boots were made to order. The bootmaker would send you literature, a short tape and instructions on how to measure your foot. You'd sit on the ground and take pains to follow the instructions and the finished boot would fit just like your foot. Simple, or it was with the bootmakers they had then. Today they don't have time."

Tony said calf-rassling and squatting on the ground kept cowhands limber enough to pull skintight boots on and off. "Hadda be limber in order to lift your foot waist high with your knee bent to get your boot off. A partner or a boot jack was a big help or I've seen guys dig their spurs into the ground and pull."

J.K. said spurs were the only way to go. "On the range you never took your spurs off at all. Just socked your spur in the ground and worked your boot off that way."

Of course the cowboy artist had some boot history for me. "Most popular boot by all odds was the Hyer, the originator of the cowboy boot. On the trail he'd ask guys what they wanted and they'd suggest this or that and he developed what came to be known as the cowboy boot, a boot with a high heel. There was probably twice as many Hyers worn by cowboys than any other boot. Justin was probably next. What I'm wearing is the best boot today, the Nokona, most like your old Hyer boot.

"You were careful to put your boot under your tarp, [because] if you get any rain inside your boot you can't put it on."

In his way, storyteller Kenny Trowbridge was as much cowboy-historian as J.K. Ralston. He told how early trail riders wore high straight-topped boots with "mule ear" straps to ease pulling the boots on. Those boots protected a rider almost to his knees. Boots became shorter as chaps became popular.

The forerunner of the modern in-laid boot was the red-topped "lone star" boot, named for its simple five-pointed–star inlay. Joe had an old pair in his closet, which were donated to the Ravalli County Museum in Hamilton, along with his big black hat, after he died. Old hands can keep on wearing hats from their cowboying days, but boots usually get put on a shelf. Bum knees and bad backs from horse injuries make it tough to pull boots on. And, even though modern boots have lower heels and shanks made for walking, they are not the most comfortable footgear to get around in (I'm asking for debate when I proclaim such a thing). Joe wore laced-up logging boots, Kenny Trowbridge had a zipper sewn into the side of his cowboy boots, Chuck Hays walked around Billings in suede, rubber-soled loafers, and Tony, except for dress, wore oxfords. J.K. stuck with his traditional cowboy boot.

J.K. Ralston, in this 1916 portrait, was wearing a pencil-curled brim on his hat—not the wide, flatter brim of his later "Boss of the Plains" style. Courtesy of Marjorie Ralston Walter

A cowhand usually had two sets of clothes, kept in his war bag. Tony said cotton, silk and wool were the basic fabrics. "I never got too hot or too cold in the heavy wool pants we used to wear. But I'm always too much one way or the other in the plastic [polyester] pants they come out with now."

Wool pants were the cowhand's first choice, and they usually wore the Pendleton brand. Tony claimed the problem with wool pants was that they were cut too high in the waist and ripped out in the crotch from the stress of horseback riding.

Tony's wife Viola sat in on most of our afternoon talks. She tried to keep out of our taped conversations, but had an interesting way of making asides.

Regarding ripped crotches, she said, "Levi solved that with the double-seamed riveted crotch. Early Levi's were guaranteed not to rip out, and were replaced if they did."

Levi's are such an American hallmark that in 1976 the Smithsonian Institution added a modern Levi suit to its Americana collection. The blue denim overall designed by Bavarian immigrant Levi Strauss in 1873 is similar to the modern jeans. Miners and farmers latched on to them first. Tony said the cowhand didn't get on the Levi bandwagon until the style was made less baggy. Early hands seldom wore belts, and Tony recalled jeans having little buckles in the back. "We were shaped different then," he said, patting his belly.

Levi's were the last item of clothing to go on in the morning, a feat possible because boots were small and sleek, not because pants were baggy. "They weren't pegged in or ballooned out, they were medium," Tony said.

The denim pants came in one length and, rather than shorten them, cowboys usually turned up the cuff. When I remarked on the six- or eight-inch cuff in some early photos of Tony, Kenny commented, "That long cuff came in mighty handy, could hang a horseshoe or put nails in it when you was shoeing, or use it fer an ashtray when ya was visitin' in someone's parlor, or jes' put odds and ends in it…"

Whether other hands squirreled away necessities in their cuffs, I cannot say. Kenny continued to wear an extra-wide cuff.

Levi's were practical, cheap, comfortable and durable. They fitted handily over a pair of longjohns or under chaps. Tony claimed he'd purchased enough Levi's to stretch in a line the nine miles from his house to mine. He said brands such as Wrangler and Lee that followed Levi appeared to be just as practical, but old-timers generally stuck with brands they started with. One of the nice things about jeans is that they adapt to fit a cowboy's changing silhouette—an old hand's belly slips

Kenny Trowbridge always wore his overalls cuffed deeply, forming extra pockets. Photo by Jo Rainbolt

nicely over the waistband. Old hands never seem to gain in the rear end, so their jeans generally bag in the seat.

White shirts were standard. "That's all we wore, and scrubbed 'em for trips to town," Tony said, adding, "If we happened to be camped along a creek, we'd tie 'em in the water for several hours."

Those were the days of no frills—white shirt, jeans, silk neckerchief, polished boots, well-brushed hat, shave and a haircut was standard for trips to town.

The drugstore cowboy was a different matter. Tony described such fellows as "all dressed up, no place to go." One such cowboy stood out in his mind. "He was newly arrived to Miles City. Apparently he had some money. He went to Al's Saddle Shop and bought a pair of fancy chaps, bat wings they were, and had some silver mountings put on 'em and conchos down the leg. He had spurs, silver-mounted spurs, bought a hat and a big neckerchief, leather gauntlets for the cuffs of his shirt—really rigged himself out. The reason I remember him so well is that he'd get decked out in the morning and walk Main Street most of the day. I don't remember how long that lasted, I guess he finally got raw-hided [teased] so much he finally gave it up, realized he was making a fool of himself."

Kenny Trowbridge gave me a copy of a photo taken in the early 1920s of himself and three young cowboy friends. Talk about dressed to the hilt—silk shirts, gauntlets, huge hats, spurs. The photo was used to advertise a national cowpuncher tour and appeared in newspapers all over the country. Joe Hughes, a close friend of Kenny's, looked at it and said, "I'm not saying Kenny wasn't a good hand, but we never looked like that."

Could it be, I asked Kenny, that you guys were spoofing onlookers in your fancy get-ups? You couldn't shoot out signposts anymore, so you swaggered. "Goddamned right!" he bawled. "We went all out. Loosened our spurs, dragged 'em along the board sidewalk so they'd go klunk, klunk…"

I never saw Kenny in anything but blue chambray or straightforward pearl-snapped cowboy shirts. He recalled owning a red silk shirt as a young hand, and said velvet was within the realm of shirt material for a young hand looking towards town. He and his pals even sported frilly garters on their sleeves and tied Charlie Russell-type sashes through belt loops. And then they klunked their spurs right down to the photography studio. Those photos from the late 1910s and early 1920s probably encouraged the myth of the dandified cowboy as much as the dime novel, and the real cowboys loved it!

Going-to-town clothing was one thing, cold-weather clothing another. Men and cattle could easily freeze to death on Montana's wintry plains. "It was easy to get a job if you could stand the winter weather," Joe Hughes said.

Joe recalled making a cross-country horseback trip to northern Montana as a young hand. He was thawing out at a ranch when the wagon boss for the Horseshoe Bar ranch came by, looking for riders. "The first thing the boss said was 'A guy willing to make a trip cross-country in this snow and cold wouldn't be as sissy as some of the guys I got down there. Every time we come out from driving cattle some of the guys don't want to come back, hole up or hide out...'"

Tom Harwood rode for that same Horseshoe Bar, and told stories about icy drives that made me shiver in July. He said he ran into two or three men who would do any camp job, even dishes, to avoid northern Montana's fierce windy winters. But "those fellas were rare. Most guys'd do anything to stay on horseback, even in winter."

Frigid temperatures didn't faze Joe. "Hell, you had clothes you could wear out or sleep out in the snow in. Most everybody had leather chaps, wore heavy wool underwear all the time, used to wear them year 'round. All-wool, ya know, [I] don't wear them much since I come into town. I used to be outdoors all the time."

Tony said most hands owned a complete set of red or black woolen underwear. "Between those and your woolie chaps, you'd do all right, long as you had a horse to carry the weight."

Woolies were heavy chaps with the hair left on the hide, designed for cold weather and okay to wear as long as a horse was carrying the load. Chaps were not items of fashion as they are nowadays. Tony was tickled about the time the eastern gal hired to clean the bunkhouse announced she'd thrown out a grimy old pair of leather pants with the seat worn out.

Some cowhands went barehanded in winter, but most wore gloves. Mittens were warmer, but didn't allow for roping. The men pulled heavy felt overshoes or oversized wool socks over their cowboy boots. Kenny Trowbridge recalled his favorite old puncher, Bill Worthington, creating a pair of burlap overshoes diaper-style. Joe had an ingenious solution to cold feet. "If it got real cold we'd wear a pair of old boots that didn't have any oil left in 'em at all. You could kick 'em in the water, freeze a coating of ice over 'em, make 'em airtight. Stick 'em in your stirrups, you could ride all day, [your] feet stay warm."

Ears and faces were protected by that most versatile of cowboy garb, the silk muffler or kerchief. "They wonder why guys got in the habit of wearing those handkerchiefs. You could pull 'em up over your face, over your ears," Joe said.

The kerchief could be tied loosely in front in a fancy knot, such as the four-cornered windowpane knot Kenny demonstrated whenever I wore a silk scarf. But its uses were mostly practical. Tony recalled using one to filter mud from creek water for a decent drink. Tied around the face bandit-style, the kerchief kept out biting wind or choking dust. In northern climates it worked better than earmuffs, tied under a hat and around the chin. Cowboys traveled light and a kerchief often was called upon for use as a sling or bandage.

Joe sometimes used a kerchief to tie his spurs on to prevent losing them from a broken strap. "If I knew I was in for some rough riding, I used to tie my spur down with a piece of stout cord or string. If I didn't have any cord, I took a handkerchief—it was silk and it was tough—tore it in two and used that. Spoiled a good handkerchief, but you do things like that."

Summer roundups were invariably hot and dusty and the most common use of the kerchief was wiping sweat from the eyes. For this reason, the kerchief was tied in back and allowed to hang loosely in front where the cowhand could grab it when needed, almost like a bib.

J.K. Ralston, my expert on such matters, said the kerchief was never draped casually over one shoulder. There was one exception, the Hollywood cowboy.

J.K. couldn't help but add, "Hollywood had to get it all wrong, right down to the kerchief."

It was more fun to ride a buckin' horse than it was to be called in fer supper.

"Wild Horse" Wes Wright

The short-lived Yellowstone Rodeo Company posed for this 1923 picture in Austin, Minnesota—where the company first went broke. Co-founder Art Wahl is fourth from right. Author's collection

Yellowstone Rodeo Company

Old hands claim there is no resemblance between riding the range and participating in a modern rodeo. Perhaps J.K. Ralston said it best—"A rodeo's on perfectly level ground. A rodeo cowboy has everything going for him—gates, horses, trainers. That's far away from a rope on the prairie, mud after rain, thousands of things to contend with."

Early rodeos, called bucking contests, matched man against horse. The event was often a Sunday afternoon affair, complete with onlookers and bets, but it could be private. Wild-Irish Donovan McGee and his young friends roped horses off the range and held informal bucking contests in empty shipping corrals between Powell and Cody, Wyoming.

"Nobody knew what we were doing. Some old rancher would get on his gentle horse, and wonder why it would break in two. We spoiled some good horses," Don said, adding that the youngest (then twelve) and craziest of those boys, Nick Knight, went on to become a world champion bronc rider. "Little Nick was a wild cat—throw him at a horse, he'd stick."

Don briefly described the evolution of the rodeo. "Each outfit had a bucking horse and a good rider. They'd get together, bet on the horse, add some wild horse races. Later, smart guys saw money in it, traveled place to place. In the early Thirties, bucking horses were developed. Rodeo clowns came in later, about the same time as Brahma bulls. Thank God they didn't have bulls in my time or I'da tried 'em."

Old cowhands don't necessarily criticize modern rodeos, but they're apt to point out the differences between then and now. The participants, for one thing. "World champion rodeo riders ain't necessarily cowboys—they kin ride, been trained like athletes, but maybe they've never worked a cow on the range," said Kenny Trowbridge.

And the horses, for another. There was no such thing as professional bucking stock in a bucking contest. A contender rode his own saddle horse (which was broken to ride and might decide against putting on much of a bucking show), or he rode a horse off the range. "Those range horses, you might compare 'em to a bull elk when you got 'em in a corral and got a rope on 'em," Tony Grace said. "They were wild, ran out the year 'round since the time they were colts. You put 'em in the corral with a loop tied around their neck, and they just bucked all over the place."

Range cattle weren't a joke, either. They were demanding, feisty critters. Roping and branding dogies during roundup was a continual rodeo, so steer roping and calf wrestling events weren't included in early rodeos. On or off the range, old-time stock was dangerous. We all know about bulls, but it was mother cows who could be truly dangerous. Lamenting the meekness of modern stock, Kenny said, "A mother no longer even fights for her calf."

Next comes the difference in attitude. Bucking-contest cowboys competed, but usually in the name of fun. "There was always the question who was the better rider, who had the better horse—those things were settled in a contest. It was fun. People got together on a Sunday and rode it out," Tony said, adding that this attitude carried over into early professional rodeos.

At the risk of romanticizing the early rodeo rider, I must relate an incident that Tony witnessed. Two closely-matched top contenders were riding for the championship. The contest was close, and when it was over, the winner handed his rival half the prize. "He knew it was luck, that either one of 'em could have won," Tony explained.

The best rodeo that Tony recalled took place at Camp Lewis, Washington, when cowboys serving in the army were training cavalry horses. "We had three men dressed in silk hats, wearing long coats with tails, and three small cowboys dressed as women with big flowing skirts—all exceptional riders. They were hauled out into the arena where six head of bucking stock were waiting. They all mounted and started at the same time. It was really funny to see those boys—those "girls," with skirts a-flowing—spurring those horses. At the same time aero bombs started exploding overhead. It was really a wild show. I rode a mule."

Tony said the contestant most respected in early rodeos was the saddle bronc rider. Skill played a big part in saddle bronc riding. "The bull rider was gutsy, but he didn't have much control over the situation."

Tony called riding broncs a "balance proposition...You have to go with him when he goes, just right, or you get bucked off. You get a kick out of it if you can stay on, I really enjoyed it. If I wasn't sure of myself it wasn't very funny. It wasn't a bit funny when you found yourself slippin' and getting out of step with the horse."

Usually, it wasn't difficult to get a horse to buck. "Very few of the old range horses that wouldn't buck at times," Tony said. "There were tricks to make 'em buck, a saddle horse could be trained to buck. Like one fella I got to know rode a great big horse, stood a good seventeen hands. A hand is four inches, fifteen [hands] two [inches] was standard for a saddle horse, so seventeen puts him up there pretty well. All he hadda do was pull a hair out of the horse's mane, and that horse bucked. Lots of little tricks like that would get a horse off."

Don McGee said he unwittingly rode Steamboat, the big black bucking horse legendary in rodeo circles from 1901 until he was put down after an injury in 1914. Very few riders managed to stay on the Wyoming-bred "King of the Bucking Horses"—whose image, some claim, adorns that state's license plate today. Steamboat was a mighty challenge to the cowboy's motto "not a horse that can't be rode..." A lucky few did manage to ride him.

Don McGee was a young boy when he said he climbed aboard the famous horse. Steamboat was lazing around a corral like an ordinary cayuse. "I didn't know a thing about him, he was just somebody's ranch buckin' horse. He didn't buck or jump with me. Then my Uncle Meryl got on. He threw [Meryl] so high I thought he was never gonna come down."

But Uncle Meryl had known Steamboat and his reputation. "Fear does it, a horse senses fear," Don explained.

Tony was a new boy when he came across his first bucking contest in the central Montana town of Roundup during its 1908 Fourth of July celebration.

He recalled it with his usual genius for detail. "A fellow named Bill Morgan bucked out his saddle horse, a buckskin and a pretty good bucking horse. He just got out there and gigged him and got him to buck. Gigging? That's spurring 'em lightly. 'Course now the rodeo horses you got, the trained buckin' stock, you don't hafta but touch 'em up there with the spurs in the shoulder and they'd blow the plug, as they say. That's no man's land up there, touchy. And the flank would be more touchy, a less often touched area.

"The other fella in the contest, Ralph Roots was his name, he rode a big old brown horse, not a saddle horse although he had been ridden…after [Ralph] bucked [the horse] out, [Ralph] sat on him among the riders there, they were just talking. It was something he shouldn't have done. The horse bucked him off right there. He rode him during the contest and got bucked off afterwards. I remember the remark he made afterwards, he said, 'I never seen it fail when a man tries to get wise'."

"Only two guys in the bucking contest?" I asked.

Tony nodded, and of course I asked who won. "I don't know if there was any prize offered."

"You mean they rode just to ride? Every person watching could decide who they thought was best? Unless a fella got bucked off and of course he was a loser?"

Tony Grace bought and saved this memorable view of Smoky Branch on Glass Eye (1923) because "I liked it— they've got him in a good position." Courtesy of Tony Grace

He chuckled, "They generally pick a coupla judges, they don't judge 'em like they do today. It's all done by sight, you watch 'em and write down your opinion and the other fella writes down his. Maybe they talk it over and decide. I think generally that's the way it's done."

Tony sat back in his easy chair, adjusting the light-shading blue visor that replaced his cowboy hat indoors. "That was my first year in Montana, 1908, and before the year was out I was in a bucking contest. I bought an old retired cow horse and he learned to buck."

It was a private bucking contest. The crew was moving cattle out of an alfalfa field near the home ranch and the hands wanted to see Tony on his bucking horse, Button. "I got on him and he didn't do a thing." Tony chuckled at the memory, "I didn't want to disappoint the boys so I reached up and I gigged him in the shoulder. He bowed his head and looked down across the barnyard and towards the irrigation ditch and he bucked along that ditch 'til he hit a fence and he doubled back and he came back up that ditch.

"I was doing all right at the time, but at one point we came to a foot bridge across the ditch and I wasn't paying any attention to it and he just side stepped onto the bridge and I zigged instead of zagged. I landed between two stones that were sticking out of the ground about [a foot]. Kinda sharp but luckily I fit right on down between 'em."

"You've been lucky, Tony, you've had some close calls," I said, a comment I was to repeat to Art Wahl when he told me about his Yellowstone Rodeo Company.

The end of World War I marked the beginning of a new era. Art came back from training cavalry stock and found mechanization was in, horses out.

Before the war, Art had been raising draft horses. He had just sold two when he got called into the Army in 1917. "They were good horses, I sold one for a hundred fifty dollars, one for a hundred twenty-five. When I come out in the spring of 1919, I had thirty head I'd left with my brother, figuring I could sell them after the war. But they were going for five dollars apiece. Even an eight-hundred-dollar stud horse would only bring five dollars," Art said.

Rather than sell his stock for nothing, Art and neighboring horse ranchers near Glendive, the Carlsburg brothers, decided to start a traveling rodeo.

"We didn't know enough about it," Art said in his soft Norwegian-accented voice.

Still, they planned it well. The three had a lot in common: they were single, broke, smart, easy-going and Norwegian. First they went to work for the Northern Pacific railroad to raise money. Next Jack Carlsburg went on the road from Montana to Wisconsin to book engagements for the Yellowstone Rodeo Company.

It wasn't difficult to find men or stock for the rodeo, mechanization coming in and a lot of cowboys out of work. Sixteen local boys were hired to ride in Art's rodeo, and good bucking stock was picked from Art's thirty head and the two or three hundred at the Carlsburg Horse Ranch.

The first stop was Grand Forks, North Dakota. "That's where we made some money," Art said. Events were mainly bucking horse rides and trick rides, such as the Roman Ride where one rider stands astride two horses. There weren't many rodeos in those days and the crowds loved it.

"It was the Fourth of July and that helped. We made four thousand dollars there—and lost it in the very next town," Art said.

Expenses were hefty. The cowboys were paid well, a hundred dollars a week. Men and stock were moved by rail.

"Sounds like fun," I said.

"We thought it was," Art replied.

"Were you in the rodeo?"

"You bet."

Austin, Minnesota is where the Yellowstone Rodeo Company went broke. "Was it raining?" I asked.

Art chuckled. "No, it was good weather. But a very small town, no customers."

The owners dug into their own pockets and shipped the outfit on to the next stop, Chippewa Falls, Wisconsin. "There we broke even," Art said.

They sent for a carload of fresh horses and went on to Superior, Wisconsin, where they went totally broke. Again, not enough customers. "Them that went enjoyed it, most of them went all three days," Art said.

It was in Superior that an amazing thing happened to Art. If I'd heard it from anyone else, I might have scoffed. It was quite a speech coming from terse Art, in his slightly lilting voice.

"One of the Kelly brothers drew this horse and was afraid of him. None of the other boys wanted him so they asked me and I said 'Sure I'll ride him.' He didn't hardly buck at all, he run across the track and right into this eight-foot fence. I saw he wasn't going to stop, I got thrown right over the fence, landed in the sixth row of the grandstand."

It sounded like the end of the story. "Did you get hurt?"

"No, not a bit. A girl sitting there in the grandstand with her boyfriend, I landed right alongside them. She was scared."

"How'd it feel to fly?"

Art laughed. "It went so fast I didn't think about nuthin'. The crowd was cheering. I got up and jumped over the eight-foot fence and then the horse was dead."

In his way, Art was a master storyteller. I was always wondering what else he had left out.

"You mean the horse was lying there dead?"

"Ya. When they seen that, then they booed me."

"Booed or not, I'd say you were a very lucky guy."

"I was lucky. I always been lucky. Never broke a bone. All my life I always had good luck, never crippled up."

"You knew how to fall, huh?"

"Mostly luck, I think."

Montanans who heard about my interest in old cowboys gave me referrals. I wasn't able to follow up on all of them up—it's a huge state and I'm as self-absorbed as every other modern American (except that the old hands' easy attitude is unwinding me). At any rate, when a friendly lady named Lois Wonder called and told me there was a "dear old rodeo clown" named Bobbie Hill living with his concert pianist wife in Paradise, I followed up on it. My daughter Kristen and I drove to the tiny town west of the Flathead Indian Reservation in northwestern Montana.

Bobbie was indeed dear. Not only his eyes, but his whole face twinkled. He told great stories, set the table and hustled up a delicious lunch for his wife, Helen, Kristen and me. Bobbie and Helen were an elfin pair, barely reaching my shoulder. Small of stature and large-hearted: a couple to remember. He was eighty-three and healthy when I met them in 1984, she a few years older and in poor health. Bobbie went to get another jar of homemade canned peaches during lunch and Helen said she never realized men could take care of people until she met Bobbie. He even warmed her flannel nightie on the space heater each night before bed.

A Canadian concert pianist from an aristocratic Scottish family, Helen spent her girlhood under the watchful eyes of servants and a patriarchal father. During her youth and middle years, she played the piano and nursed her invalid mother. At age forty-four, she met and married Bobbie, a veteran rodeo clown.

Helen was a natural comic, but she didn't compete or even make a bid for attention. The only thing she told me directly about her life was, "I think I've been a sissy." While I tape recorded Bobbie, Helen sat next to Kristen on the sofa and whispered stories about her own past in Kristen's ear.

I gave Bobbie a general idea what I was interested in—his background, how he got into rodeo and clowning (most clowns were excellent rodeo riders), funny experiences. His eagerness to talk was touching. And could he talk! Stories rolled out of him. His life is the story of early rodeo.

"I was born in Boston in 1901 and lived in Philadelphia as a toddler. Used to go to Atlantic City on summer vacations, big old wooden boardwalk and the beautiful beaches, ya know. My biggest event was riding on the merry-go-round. My sister set me up on the horse, she'd be standin' beside me and you'd come by an arm that had a brass ring on it. She'd catch the brass ring and give it to me and I'd try to throw it in a big clown's mouth. So I guess from the time I was three years old it was clowns and horses connected.

"My parents split up when I was still little and I moved to Philadelphia and on to Washington, D.C. with my mother, sister and aunt. My playground was the Capitol and the tunnels under the Capitol steps. I used to ride my tricycle all over. If you did that today somebody'd shoot you.

"My first experience with horses was in Gary, Indiana. We moved there when I was about ten. The produce man delivered in a two-wheel cart and we used to get up on the cart.

Bobbie Hill (emerging from the barrel) in his days as a rodeo clown. Author's collection

"In 1914, my parents got back together some way and I was living in Edmonton [Alberta] where my dad was in the work horse business. He handled farm machinery, buggies, wagons. He had three saddlemakers working for him all the time. The barn—I don't know how many horses it held but it was over a hundred feet long with stalls on both sides, you could ride a four-horse team right down the middle.

"'Course I took right to the horses. We had saddle horses and good driving horses. He wouldn't rent a horse, he sold horses. I was jumping horses when I was fifteen, sixteen. These guys ridin' a jumping horse today go over a hurdle about this high, we used to ride fourteen [hand], two[inch] ponies over four-foot, two hurdles. I'd have a twelve-hundred-pound pulling horse to ride today and a Shetland pony tomorrow. We went to a lot of horse shows. When I was about fifteen I won a little silver medal. In 1919, I won a gold medal riding a flat saddle. I cowboyed but I never forgot how to ride English.

"Kind of a little laugh about that. I was working for a big cow outfit up in British Columbia in 'thirty-seven. They had a hundred thousand acres fenced, seven thousand head of cattle. The owner's wife had a horse the doctor was going to come out and take a look at and wanted me to ride him first. She said, 'You ever ride a flat saddle?' I said, 'Yes, I rode a flat saddle.' I got up and wheeled this horse around, she said, 'Where'd you learn to ride like that? You've got good hands and feet.' You never heard anybody in the West talk about hands and feet in connection with a horse. I said, 'I learned to ride like that a long time ago.'

"I attended a private school in Edmonton, [where] every new boy had a review. Believe it or not, I could write two full pages on Canadian history and never look at the book. I finished school, should have gone further but I was tired of it, went down south to Calgary to work on a place, came back to Edmonton that fall and from then on I just went from horse to horse.

"Rodeoing and me dates way back. I wanted to learn trick roping from the time I was in Gary, Indiana and saw a guy trick ropin' in a theater. I braided a piece a rope and got started. Saw another trick roper when I was a kid, went to the North

Ever the performer, Bobbie Hill posed with the author's five-foot, three-inch daughter Kristen Schloemer in 1984. Photo by Jo Rainbolt

American Cabaret in Chicago one night for supper, there was a fella there trick roping. When I went to Edmonton in 1914 I met a fella named Johnny Barry and his sister Violet. They were performers in circuses, rodeos, and they started me out with a key, just like you're learning to play the piano. And I just went on from there, up and up, and got pointers from different people.

"In 'twenty-one and 'twenty-two I started going to what they called small stampedes. In the summer of 'twenty-five my first wife, Hazel, and I traveled fifteen hundred miles with eighty head of horses and teams and wagons, following the stampedes. I competed for years before I clowned. Did trick ropin', trick ridin', mostly I rode saddle and bareback horses.

"I played to some of the big ones. First clownin'—I never dressed up or nuthin', I could always find something to say when something happened. Ad-libbing. You work with announcers today and ninety-nine percent have to have something to read, they can't ad lib. Jack Benny, Bob Hope, all those boys, if they couldn't ad lib—why, that's what made them.

"Wanted somebody years ago to create something different from ad libbing and just a talkin', so I went to clowning. I just wore the big pants and chin whiskers and white hair. Had a two-wheel cart with a goose neck behind it, we used to ride behind that...I'd take a big scoop shovel, tie a rope on a horse's tail, tie it just once, ride that scoop shovel and when you turned the rope loose you turned the scoop shovel loose.

"I could run a cow or steer down afoot. After somebody got bucked off, I'd run and grab the tail and sit down. If they turned around to git ya, couldn't git ya.

"Worked on tour for Cisco Kid in 'fifty-six and 'fifty-seven, I was his 'old prospector.' Got shot twice a day but I lived through it. I can name the states I haven't been in better than the ones I have been in, and I been in every province in Canada. I've worked Calgary, Montreal, Winnipeg, Vancouver, Los Angeles, New York.

"We always closed the show with a fightin' bull—that held the crowd. I'd work in the barrel, the other fella'd be outside. When the chute was empty we'd tell the crowds, 'Okay, goodbye,' and the announcer would say, 'Hey, wait a minute we got something for you.' They'd carry two bulls, nuthin' but fighting bulls. We'd fight one bull, get ready to go, the announcer'd say, 'Oh no, we got somethin more for you.' And we'd fight the other.

"Today's rodeo's gone so modern and commercial, it's different. If they had everybody register and vote on what they like the most, I'd say eighty percent of the public is buying entertainment. That's why we put the bull fighting last, people liked it."

Everything's in your way when you're boogered up.

J.K. Ralston

Tony Grace noted that bucking bull Sharkey—here unloading an un-
wanted and unnamed rider—had loose skin and was impossible to ride
with a saddle. "They learned," he said. It was only one of many ways to
get hurt. Courtesy of Tony Grace.

Handpainted Guts

Most of the old hands I know suffered serious horse-related accidents, and the incidents always seemed to happen too far to fetch a doctor. Some, like Charles "Doc" Williamson, who broke his femur in high country and lay alone two weeks to recuperate, were crippled later in life. Joe Hughes was luckier. Before his marriage to gentle Pearl, his wild-Irish streak almost did him in. He suffered bizarre illnesses and freak accidents, but he lived to relate the details.

My notes indexing a single tape-recording of Joe's reminiscences paint a picture of teenaged Joe far from home, and accident-prone. At inch number 219: Joe's horse drowned. Inch 250: Busted up in Deer Lodge by horse in stall; developed typhoid fever, spent July–Nov. in hosp., passed 17th birthday alone there. Inch 285: Broke his neck breaking a horse in spring 1911, discovered on X-ray 60 years later.

That particular tape now is in the archives at the University of Montana. I imagine a future scholar raising an eyebrow over that last entry, but it was quite logical the way Joe told it:

"I went home in November after getting out of the hospital but had a fall-out with my father and left a few days before Christmas. Went to work for a guy, he was tryin' to break a horse by puttin' a sack over its head, in the barn. 'Course I hadda speak up, no way to treat a horse. And I ended up gettin' on the horse—which you should never do in a barn—got out okay but the horse slipped on a patch of ice, threw me headfirst into a post."

"Ouch. What did you do then, go to a doctor?"

"No, I just carried my head cocked to one side, can't recall which side, one side to the other it laid over. I couldn't straighten my neck most of the winter, but I could still work, drive a team."

"Didn't it hurt?"

"Hurt like hell. I used to rub and twist it, try to straighten it. I knew it was kinked or hurt, but I never knew it was broke. It did straighten up towards spring."

"How'd you find out you'd broken it?"

"About a year after Pearl and I come to town, why my neck started hurtin' me and I thought it was from cocking my head sideways, watching TV. Started paining, hurt like the devil. I had to carry it twisted again. So I went to the doctor, first thing they did was X-ray it, he said, 'When did you break your neck, Joe?'"

"When was this?"

"Gosh, it musta been in the Fifties. Sometime like that. No, it was later. Musta been sixty years when he discovered it. Put it in a neck brace for awhile. Let's see, it happened in 1911, this guy made me so sore, he was supposed to be a bronc rider..." And Joe elaborated on the unfair methods the fella was using to break the horse that broke Joe's neck.

Old hands never blame the horse.

Horses don't overreact on purpose. Tony said few are born outright ornery, but surprise or injury or confusion makes them act that way. "The first time a horse taught me a lesson," Tony began, "I walked into a stall and he didn't hear me. On the ground was three or four inches of dried manure, you could walk on it without making any noise. I wanted to get him and saddle him up, his head was down in the manger. He lifted his head and saw me beside him and it startled him. He backed me against the wall and jumped up like he wanted to kick. I kept talking to him, his name was Prance, 'Easy, Prance, don't you do it,' stuff like that. He finally calmed down and stepped aside. He had me pinned to the wall, he could have really poured it on. Always speak to a horse, even when he sees you."

His wife Viola chimed in, "Well, you startle a person when you come up like that, too." I thought of all the times I've wanted to whomp someone for startling me.

"Wild Horse" Wes Wright peered at me through his gold-rimmed glasses and described the sensation of getting hung up in the stirrup by the sole of a thick felt overshoe, so I asked the required question, "You ever been dragged by a horse?"

"I been drug quite a few times. I've had horses buck me off and hang me up on the stirrup, and drag and kick me 'til my boot come off." His eyes danced behind thick lenses. The cowboy who referred me to Wes described him as the biggest-hearted, craziest horseman in the Bitterroot Valley. And, the cowboy added, Wes had more horse-sense than ten modern cowboys. Wes liked to describe himself as "half-horse."

I asked why Wes walked stiff-kneed, and he related the following incident. It happened in 1957, when Wes was already in his fifties.

"I had a horse slip and fall and I was hung up in the stirrup. There was a fella with me. He didn't see the horse fall but he seen me after the horse got up and I was hung up and horse was kickin' me. He kicked me in the face, broke my nose, kicked all my teeth loose—my face was just a battered-up mess. I was knocked out, didn't know a thing about it. Knocked me cold when [the horse] slipped, he fell hard, the ground was kinda slick. I laid there and slept for about four hours.

"[My companion] didn't know where to go for help—new in the country—he stayed there with me 'til I woke up. When I woke up I knew my leg was broke and I sent him for help to get me to town...seventy miles...Roads bad, car bumpin' all over, longest seventy miles I ever rode.

"When I got there my leg was so swelled up [they] couldn't set it, hadda put me in traction....Stuck a pin right through my leg and put a traverse on it just above the knee, and put me in a high bed with a pulley on it with a weight and a rope runnin' through this traverse and through that pulley. Hung that weight over the foot of the bed, and I just hadda push with this other foot to keep from goin' outa bed, and I laid like that for fifteen days before the swelling went down so they could set it.

"I told the doctor to pick my teeth [out] and throw 'em away. (I had my own teeth then.) He said, 'Oh, they'll grow back in,' but they never did. I hadda get false teeth. My face healed, but my nose is still crooked. It was worse, leanin' way over to one side."

J.K. Ralston was riding home in the dead of night after courting his sweetheart, the pretty schoolteacher named Willo who became his wife. It was cold, a wintry night, with patches of snow on the ground. One of the patches had a hole under it. "The horse ran his right foreleg into that hole and down we went. I didn't have a chance to do a thing. 'Course it was the dead of winter and the edge of the hole was frozen solid just like the inside of a barrel. My leg got right in the hole with his leg, and snapped both bones above the ankle. I knew it was broken when I got up—which is hard to do on one leg in the middle of the night—and nuthin' hurt and my foot spun around."

J.K.'s horse was untouched by the fall. "Didn't take him long to get to his feet, he stood there and waited for me. Didn't take me long 'til I didn't need a horse anymore, no way to stand on one leg and mount a horse. That's an odd feeling, I got down on all fours and I kept sayin', 'You damn fool, why don't you get up and walk?' 'Walk on what?' I got crawlin' away and my horse stayed with me, a coupla hundred feet away. He happened to look around and see me and nuthin' else. Boy, he thought I was a bear or somethin'. I can still hear him snort. Then he took off on a dead run."

J.K. had about a half mile to crawl through a field. He got into it. "You have to find out what you're capable of doing and what you can't do. One of the first things I found out was that I had to keep my foot straight up and down, that kept it in one piece, otherwise the bones would grind against each other. You reach as far ahead as you can with one leg, then draw the other one up to ya."

A cow bawled, and J.K. was frightened for the first time that evening. "It occurred to me all at once when I heard that cow that just out of sight around a bend was where the neighbor fed his cattle. It struck me that if the cows saw me up there on all fours I was in trouble. You see, first it's curiosity—they gather 'round—then purty soon one of 'em will take a butt at ya. Yuh, that's exactly what would happen to ya, and boy I crawled for a long long ways with my heart in my mouth, afraid one would see me, but none showed up. You don't dare do anything like that, cattle will attack anything like that. You know how they'll run a dog, it's the same. They don't even know what you are. If you were able to even get up and stand on one foot it's not likely they'll pay attention for very long. Well, I made it as far as the ranch house, about three quarters of a mile."

Despite permanent injury from a horse early in life, Charles "Doc" Williamson (shown in 1981) was a Bitterroot Valley veterinarian and author of a horse training book sold around the world.
Photo by Jo Rainbolt

The accident happened around 10:30 at night and a doctor couldn't be found until 2:30 the following afternoon. "By that time it was giving me a purty good time. He set it with splints. We both knew it was broken, [and] I tried to tell him it was out of joint, too."

J.K. came up with a statement I've heard time and again from old hands, one that modern medicine is finally trying out: "A doctor oughta listen to a patient."

It wasn't long before J.K. was hobbling

around, visiting his sweetheart, but a sore foot is a lot more vulnerable than a sore thumb. "Everything's in your way when you're boogered up," is how the poet-artist put it, adding, "There could be forty-five people there and you're the one who'll get it."

J.K. ended up with one leg shorter than the other. "I could never stroll like other people; one day I figured out you have to have even legs." But he figured he was lucky. "I had hurts from a horse falling, but I was lucky enough not to have one of 'em go into a hole like that again."

Quick thinking and ingenuity ranked first when accidents happened far from help, and cowboys were known to possess both. The most original cowboy treatment I've heard was described to Mary Welte by her husband, Clarence, and sixty years later passed on to me.

It happened in cold north country near the Bears Paw Mountains. By tradition in this country, cowboys galloped away from schoolhouse dances in high spirits, whooping like crazy and brandishing firearms. Trouble was, barbed wire fences were already a part of the West when a young cowhand rode right into one. Mary said the gash was so severe that the fellow's intestines were torn out. The other hands figured him for a goner, but nevertheless acted quickly, wrapping him in a water-soaked, gaudily colored soogan, and riding forty miles toward the nearest doctor. The cowboy lived. The doctor who sewed him up said the cowboy had "the only hand-painted guts in Montana." The home-dyed quilt had transferred bright designs onto his innards.

And then there is Tom Harwood's story of being dragged by a horse for more than twenty-four hours, and living to tell about it. I know it sounds unbelievable, what they call a "big windy," but it's true. Tom didn't even consider it worth telling until the health subject came up while he was talking about breaking horses. "Last one I broke was about ten years ago, I was about seventy-three—had to slow down after I had that heart attack, broke the sac around the heart and they told me to slow up on some of that horse stuff...so I cut her down a little bit."

"You ever had any horse accidents?" I asked.

"Just one. I had an albino—boy, that was a pretty thing. Pure white. Some are kinda moon-eyed, imagine they see somethin' but they don't, but I hadn't noticed that on her. She bucked me off one time and kicked me on top of the head here. She threw me, when she come back over me was when she kicked me. Got mad, I guess. I seen her comin' but too late, couldn't get outa the road. I still got the mark on my head, that was the worst I had."

Tom was one of the few old-timers who kept up the smoking habit, and I watched the ash on his cigarette get longer and longer until he paused to flick it off. As an afterthought, he said, "That time I got drug, that was a bad one. Drug me from about ten-thirty in the morning until the next day at one o'clock. Through those brown cactuses, ya know—the ground wasn't plowed up."

"What happened?"

"He started buckin'...I was still hung up in the stirrup. I dunno what happened. I kinda come out of it once, I don't know if it was the evening or the next morning—but he was played out, he wasn't runnin', he was kinda circlin' me and I was on the inside. The reins hadn't broke off him yet and I caught that inside rein and had sense enough to wrap it around my wrist and hang unto it, so it kept him in a little circle. I went out again, you see, and when they found me I was plumb out. My head hurt."

Tom pounded hard on the table to a waltz beat, THUMP, THUMP, THUMP. "...felt like this table for two days afterwards, and my eyes was swelled shut."

"Otherwise you were okay, no bones broken?"

"Bones? No bones were broken. How old was I? Oh, I was probably around 24, along in there. Before that when I got bucked off I always landed clean. The horse'd either throw me away from him or I'd get away from him some way. Some of the topnotchers, though, got hurt pretty bad."

Tom and Tony both related stories of accidents that almost happened, both under icy winter conditions. Tom, when he was a young foreman for the Horseshoe Bar outfit, had to move 2,500 head of cattle just before Christmas. A heavy snow came down during a warming trend, and then a cold snap added a crust on top, making the worst kind of snow for moving cattle.

"Darn old cattle walkin' through that. It was about belly-deep. There was two steers—a big rocky-faced one and a big kinda lined-back steer—those two took the lead and held it all the way. Them two steers never quit. Twenty-five hundred steers, one right behind the other, made quite a string, I'll tell ya. I see them old boys out there leading the stock, once in a while they'd lift a leg up and shake it, get the blood off."

But the worst part was yet to come. The weather had been temperate until the storm came, and the Two Medicine River flowing east out of Glacier National Park wasn't quite frozen.

"I had a guy from Cut Bank cooking, name o' Chuck Sanders. He said, 'I don't think we can get the wagon across, the ice won't hold up.' We hadda get across some way, so I said, 'If you hang on to my horse I'll put the wagon across.' I knew the team of horses cuz I drove 'em so goldarned much, a little team of sorrels. God, they were good horses.

"When I got ahold of that wagon, I made a big circle, and when I hit the creek I was on a dead run. Hit that ice, my horses a-skatin' and a-skiddin'. But they're still agoin' and, by golly, the main current was to the east side just before ya went up the bank and, by God, just one wheel broke through that ice. They had enough speed and the leaders had got on the ground by that time and we got across."

When the cattle were finally coaxed across, the first bunch broke through the ice and opened up the river, making it possible to wade.

"That was quite a deal," Tom said.

While Tom told that story, his neighbor, a tired-looking man in his thirties or forties, had joined us in Tom's kitchen. He obviously enjoyed Tom's stories. And Tom, an elder of the Blackfeet tribe and great-grandson of a chief, didn't bat an eye when the neighbor asked, after the ice story, "Did ya ever have any trouble with the Indians back in them days?"

"No, about half the cowboys were Indians anyhow. Good cowboys, every one of 'em," Tom replied.

Tony's list of near-misses was impressive. A horse's kick directly in his solar plexus knocked him down while he was showing horses to French buyers during World War I in Chicago. "A cowboy picked me up. Another one said, 'Put him down,' so he dropped me." Tony was unhurt.

Another time he stood up and walked away after his galloping horse stepped in a chuck hole. "This horse liked to race—once they've been raced they can never stand to see another horse in front of them. This one stepped in a hole while running and threw me, landing [me] with my head between the horse's back legs."

It wasn't uncommon for cowboys to drown. Cattle had to be led across swollen rivers, and even a simple task like going for the mail could mean fording a river on horseback in those days.

J.K., who taught horses to swim the Missouri River when he was a kid, said he never knew a horse that couldn't pick up the art of swimming, but they were likely to panic when confronted with new water. He claimed a big river not only looked but also smelled different from the creeks a horse had drunk from all his life.

At age 101, Tony recounted how he almost died young in the Tongue River near Miles City when soft ice collapsed under his horse. It was a close call. And the summer following that incident, he saw a friend, Billy Hawkins, drown within two miles of the same spot. Hawkins' horse spooked and just pawed at the water. "Billy looked down at the water and his head disappeared. His hat went on down the river."

Tony sat for a moment, eyes looking back. "The next thing I knew, I was cutting off his boots."

Hell, you can tell jes' by lookin' at him or lookin' at one of his paintings that he's been there.

Kenny Trowbridge on J.K. Ralston

J.K. Ralston in about 1984. Photo by Jo Rain-bolt

Pictures Talking Back

As a kid, J.K. Ralston was either in the saddle or painting and drawing horses and cowboys. Ranching and art seemed to run in his family.

That family became westerners when J.K.'s grandfather moved his wife and first child from the culture and comfort of plantation life in Missouri to the wild West in the late 1850s.

"They joined a wagon train and by ox team headed west," J.K. said. "...My grandmother learned to lead team, my father learned to walk [by toddling] around the water keg along the trail. My family ended up ranching, but they didn't start out that way. Hell, nobody came to ranch. They came for gold. If there was grass they stayed and got into the ranching business. You get into cattle you gotta feed 'em—so you follow the grass. That's always been the story from start to finish—gold was what brought 'em here, grass was what kept 'em."

J.K. said a person once bitten never recovers from the gold bug. His rancher-father followed grass and gold. J.K., youngest of five children, was born March 1, 1896, in the pleasant ranching community of Choteau in northwestern Montana, but the family didn't stay in one place very long. "My father moved the family to the gold fields of British Columbia for a while. We'd been around Canada, Washington, all over the place..."

The place that most influenced the budding artist was Montana's wide-open Missouri River country. His father had given up on gold and followed the grass almost to North Dakota. J.K. was twelve and ready for action when the family settled in this cowboy heaven. He was quick to note he wasn't a "real cowboy," but he did the work of one, staying out on the trail for days with the roundup crew, gathering cows for the Pot Hound Pool.

"Big ranchers formed an association to gather cattle, called it the Pot Hook Pool, [then] some wag tagged it Pot Hound—there was a sayin' in those days, 'You ain't nuthin' but a pot hound'—and of course the name took."

J.K. took to the life of a cowhand, and older hands treated the kid well. "I always looked up to the oldtimers, never had reason to be sorry." Young J.K. took it all in: chuck wagon humor, tasty biscuits, salty language, spoiled horses, ornery cows, rain and sleet, boredom, exhilaration. It was raw material for poems and paintings that came later.

In his book, *Rhymes of a Cowboy,* is this one:

The cowboy was my hero when I was just a kid,
to me, romance and glamour stood for everything he did...

J.K. used the word cowboy, but he didn't like the modern interpretation, as I learned when I met him in 1981. Michael Korn, director of the Montana Folk Life Project, and I were gathering cowboy poems and songs for a record. western artist Stan Lynde (creator of the comic strips "Rick O'Shay" and "Latigo") sent us to J.K., describing him as the most savvy oldtimer in the state. Stan said J.K. liked to visit but I was still a little nervous about knocking on his door. "He's a famous artist, perhaps he likes to be left alone," I whispered to Mike as I saw the old hand make his way to the door.

J.K., tall, lean, hawk-eyed, looked down at me, *"Cowboys?* You want to hear stories and poems about *cowboys?* We never called ourselves that, we were filly chasers, ranahans, cowhands, anything but that goddamned term cowboy which brings to mind Hollywood's sad notion...."

The hawk look softened. "So you wanna talk? I guess you better come on in..." Our early evening session lasted until midnight. I'd known Joe Hughes for a decade by then, and I'd recently met Tony Grace (who explained things to me) and Art Wahl (who lived out the life of a silent but observant cowhand), but in that single evening the cowboy's own story was given to me by J.K. As Mike and I listened, J.K. painted vivid word pictures, but mostly the story was told through his poetry.

"Those poems came straight from my heart, stored there since I was a kid," he said after reciting his favorite poem, "Dawn in a Cow Camp."

At age twelve, J.K. had painted his first oil. He was almost as interested in Indians as in cowboys, and this first painting shows an Indian standing on the cliffs of the Missouri River. "Looking for Buffalo" now hangs in J.K.'s log cabin studio in Billings. It was painted on the back of a piece of oilcloth.

"My mother painted. She didn't create—she painted flowers and, if she liked a picture, she might copy it. I was trying to paint with her oils on paper and she said 'Why, you can't paint on that,' started lookin' around for something that would work and got this piece of oilcloth."

"Was the rest of your family artistic?" I asked.

He thought for a few minutes. "Well, my brother Frank was a damn good artist, way ahead of me. For some reason he gave it up and I kept going. Billy used to do some art work, too—he went in for cartoon stuff. I believe Allen did, too. In school a long time ago, if you had an art class, everybody was an artist. Maybe it was only once a week, or once a month, but they were all artists. Yes, my family was artistic, no doubt about it. My sister Beth was an elocutionist and could really sing. Frank, he could draw as good a buckin' horse as anybody I ever saw."

"Was he as good as Charlie Russell?"

"Nobody was as good as Charlie Russell," J.K. replied with finality.

He saw his first exhibition of Russell's work as a schoolboy in Helena in 1903 (one of the places his family lived) and never got it over it. "My first inspiration in drawing was Charlie Russell. Wallace Coburn was *the* western writer, Russell *the* artist. There'll never be another Charlie Russell."

The old artist sighed, "Just my luck to never meet him. My father knew all those fellas, especially the Coburns. A neighbor of ours, Bill McDonney, wintered with Russell and Con Price. Con Price was a great bronc rider, ya know....I knew all those fellas and of course I wanted to meet Charlie Russell. My father was gonna take us to meet him in 1903 and the studio was closed, nobody there. That was the first time. After that he was always out of town or something."

J.K decided to go to the Chicago Art Institute in 1917 when a girl named Melba visited the ranch and told him about it.

"A nice thing was, you could ride the cow train there without any money, that always helps. I made about four trips with the cattle. When my money ran out, I'd come back to Montana and work cattle for a while."

J.K. said he didn't actually ride with the cattle, or even near them. "You could ask some stockman if you could get on with his cattle at the shipping point in Culbertson, and if he said yes you were on. The railroad does all the work, they feed and do everything like that..."

It was pretty classy during the first leg of the trip. "They gave you a coach out of Culbertson, an obsolete coach no longer in service but you had the whole thing—everything that had been there in the good old days was there. It was all ours, rarely was a boy alone, you had some cowpuncher with you that had been there maybe several times. You could take yourself a cushion and make yourself a bed with two more cushions. But they took that away from you at the Twin Cities. From then on it was the caboose. That was pretty rough riding. You just used your overcoat or whatever you had with you for a blanket and put your head on your suitcase."

Upon arriving in Chicago, J.K. was amazed at the elegance of the railroad hotel, about as far from a caboose as one could go. "The old Stockyards Inn. It wasn't far from the stockyards. It was a beautiful old hotel, all done in

England, beautiful paintings and everything in it. Quite a fuss when they tore it down not too many years ago, lot of people in Chicago wanted it kept. Railroad company or whoever owned it tore it down anyway. I think it would be safe to say thousands of stockmen put up at that Stockyards Inn."

J.K. doesn't recall applying at the Art Institute. "I don't even remember that I'd made any arrangements. I don't think I'd even written 'em. Anyway, I got in."

Being at the Art Institute wasn't hard to take. J.K. found he was his own boss, just as on the range. "It's pretty much up to you, nobody checked on you, there was no calling of class or that sort of thing. You wanna fool your time away, that's your hard luck."

His first lesson was that there was nothing to learn concerning his favorite subject. "My whole bent was the West. I wasn't interested in anything else. This might sound boastful but I was the only one who knew anything about western art. Forever they were tellin' me about some bird that had been there last year was a western artist, and all this and that, but I was the only one at the time. You decided what you wanted to do, they didn't teach how to draw animals, they might have one class for a certain length of time if enough students asked for it. I didn't do western art in class; whatever the class was doing, I did. I did do it in my room, and once in a while I'd play hooky."

While we talked in the pleasant study of his daughter Marjorie Walter's Missoula home, surrounded by J.K.'s paintings and drawings, it was obvious that the old artist was making a thoughtful journey into his past. "I'd go as long as my money held out, go home and work awhile. I imagine I could have stayed away ten years, gone back there and got my outfit and walked into class. That's the reason the school was so popular and so loved, it helped so many people. They didn't throw fellas like me outa there."

Initially, J.K. was disappointed that he couldn't study his chosen subject, but it didn't take him long to realize that if he was drawing, he was learning. "For one thing, I don't think I'd ever drawn a girl in my life, and down there you get all these models..." he stopped, snorted a laugh, "Lemme tell you a little story about that."

J.K. preferred the Chicago Art Institute to the Chicago Academy of Fine Arts because, he said, "they ruled over you at the Academy." However, when the United States became involved in World War I, J.K. and his roommate decided to attend both schools before they were called to serve. "We decided we'd cram a little, go to the Academy of Fine Arts at night. We went over there to register and they accepted us all right; one of the instructors showed us through the academy. He stopped at one of the fountains to get a drink of water and as he bent over said, 'There's a class in there, just open the door and go on in.'

"I opened the door and walked in and here was the most beautiful painting that I'd about ever seen. Full life size, the frame, the whole thing. I stood there looking at it, thought, 'My gosh, what a beautiful job that is.' It was a nude painting. Over at the Institute in those days we didn't have nude models for class. So I was just standing there looking at this beautiful painting and just then the instructor came in and stood there looking for a moment beside me, you know, and all at once he said 'REST!' and the girl walked down out of the picture. Damnest shock I ever had in my life."

Ralston's log cabin studio in Billings.
Photo by Jo Rainbolt

By this time in our friendship, J.K. and I had shared some good laughs, but this one topped them all. He couldn't let go of the memory. "The idea was the frame and all, to make it like a picture." He paused, wiped his eyes and continued, still chuckling. "A true story—she walked right out of the picture."

The Institute soon introduced nude models. "I served with Uncle Sam. When I got back they'd already changed it and all life classes were in the nude. So they kept modernizing it like everything else. One of the reasons for nudity in art is to teach you anatomy, you can see the joints, the actions and all those kinds of things."

J.K. paused. "'Course it made it interesting, too."

Old cowboys generally don't put much stock in education. "An educated fool, his thoughts just came in herds," is a line from the popular song "Strawberry Roan." Pardon me: It's not education they scoff at, it's schooling. Tony, the most uncritical person I know, commented after meeting a member of the local professional elite, "Another with lots of schooling but very little education."

As far as I can tell, J.K.'s attitude towards art school had little or nothing to do with schooling. I place it firmly in the same category as Tony's trek to

Chicago to break horses for French cavalry forces or Joe's migration to eastern Montana to live with the Crow Indians. It was an experience, and it was fun. J.K. wasn't concerned with degrees. He traveled back and forth by cattle train from roundup work in Montana to art classes in Chicago until he figured he'd learned enough. Sixty years later he wasn't even sure he'd learned much; he said the work of Charlie Russell and early days on the range had been his real teachers. But he valued the time in school for the experience. "Anytime, I'd say to anybody, if you have a chance to go to a good art school, go. It broadens you, you see things differently."

J.K. followed art as his father followed gold. He supported his good-natured wife Willo and two children with his work. As Kenny Trowbridge said, "To raise a family by just painting, by Jesus, there was damn few that could do it. You had to be a good artist to raise your family by just usin' your art."

Actually, J.K. did more than paint. He followed what he called the "art game," working at commercial art in Spokane and other cities. "The one thing I always had, didn't matter what type art I was in, I could draw. I had that like most people can write on paper, same thing. So there was never any question with me to get a job as far as drawing was concerned."

J.K. did a lot of sculpture in his earlier years. "The reason I don't have it is because it was done with native Montana clay and it all broke up finally. I do have two bronzes at home, two buffalo bull and a buffalo cow and calf."

The old cowboy had done paintings, drawings, sculpture, murals. His work is exhibited in public buildings, art galleries and private homes around the world. "Do I have a first love as far as my art is concerned?" he pondered. "Well, that isn't easy to answer in that all at once you get a hot notion that you wanna model for a while and you get all hot and bothered about that and set everything else away. Then one day all of a sudden you get a hot notion that you wanna paint, maybe you've seen something or something happened and you think 'I gotta get that down right now.' That's the only way I can answer that. It's just what strikes you at the time. And there is a time when you don't want to do anything. You've gotta have that notion to go in order to go."

J.K. had little to say about other western artists. "I never made it my business to keep track of other artists. I do like to talk to 'em, sometimes artists come by, you know. There's been a lot of good western artists but I will say this—and it's true—there's been a lot of copying of Charlie Russell."

To old cowhands, Charlie Russell is western art. He painted and drew as he saw it, and what he saw was true. Poetry, songs and paintings were all the same—in order to work they had to be accurate. In order to be accurate, the artist or poet or storyteller had to have lived the experience.

"Russell had been there," Kenny Trowbridge explained. "No doubt in my mind, and you can talk to any of the old fellers, Russell was the tops. When he painted a picture, anybody that knowed the outfit could tell what horse it was or what person was on the horse. He painted scenery and stuff so they could tell what ranch it was. He could paint Indians, he could paint an old log cabin out there with a dirt roof. He painted what he knew. I think I seen a picture or two he tried to paint of buildings and nice cities and stuff and they just wasn't there."

Before settling down in 1904 to a wife, a home and a log cabin studio in Great Falls, Russell worked as a cowhand. "He warn't no bronc peeler, but he could ride good enough," Kenny said.

Working hands appreciated Russell; he told a great yarn, he wasn't above taking a snort or branding a dogie, he captured their lives and landscapes. The vast, still, unpredictable beauty of the cowboy's country and the freedom of cow camp would at least be preserved on canvas. Russell mourned over what we were losing, without being sappy about it. He showed the same sensitivity to the Indians, and what they already had lost. A large mural of his hangs in Montana's capitol, documenting Lewis and Clark's first meeting with the Salish Indians (which took place in the Bitterroot Valley, not far from where Tony and Kenny and I settled). But this painting tells the story from the Indians' point of view, and they are the featured figures in the foreground.

No wonder every other old cowboy in the state claims to have met him. "Guys who weren't even dry behind the ears when Russell was too old to ride say they were partners with him," Joe Hughes snorted. But the cowboy-artist with the ready wit and downhome ways really did get around. Callie Billings was no more than a kid in 1910, riding herd during the last buffalo roundup, when he came across a friendly cowpoke in a canvas tipi wearing a colorful sash. In his sash and rumpled clothes, Charlie went where the action was. Paul Young saw him sitting on a fence drawing bucking broncs while Paul was breaking horses for the cavalry in Miles City in 1912. Art Wahl spotted him in a Great Falls saloon. "What'd he look like?" Art shrugged at my question, "Mm, like an old cowboy."

It wasn't until Tom Harwood offhandedly mentioned some advice Charlie Russell gave to Tom's artistic brother Bill that I met an old hand who actually knew Russell.

"Charlie Russell must have been a neat guy, do you remember him?" I asked Tom. By neat I meant interesting, as in "whatta guy." Tom thought I meant tidy.

"Oh yuh. Well, he always took care of himself, but he was kinda trashy-lookin'. He wore an old sash, ya know, all the time. It was tied around his belly, half a knot in it, hung down both ends. 'Course he dressed kinda cowboyish-like. Always wore boots and a Stetson hat."

"Everybody seemed to like him…"

"He was a good guy. I liked old Charlie. He was a very interesting fellow to be with. I and Paul were down there [in Great Falls] one time, and we went to visit old Charlie in his log cabin. Paul was tellin' a story about Dad. Dad knowed Charlie Russell all his life, before Dad was ever married. Dad always worked on big outfits and horse roundups and everytime they had one of them Charlie Russell would go out there, that's where he got his idea on that western scenery."

"So Paul was telling a story about your Dad?"

"Yuh. The old man was out on a roundup one morning when a horse bucked so hard or one thing and another, kind of waltzed him, and the old man was supposed to take the whomp outa him. I guess he put on quite a show out there on this gray horse, and so anyhow, Paul started to tell the story and he said, 'Oh, heck, Charlie, I can't tell it the way you do. You tell it.' Will Rogers was there, he was visitin' with Charlie, old Will Rogers. So anyhow, Charlie started to tell the story then, 'Oh heck,' he said and reached over for a piece of paper and a pen and he said, 'I can draw the picture of him quicker than I can tell the story.' So he drawed this picture…you couldna taken a better picture with a Kodak. 'Course he could draw horses and the old man's face was just like you woulda took it with a Kodak. He wrote on the back of it, turned it over and wrote 'Compliments to Tom Harwood from Charlie Russell,' and dated it."

"And Will Rogers was there too?"

"Yuh, I liked him. It was better'n any picture show sittin' back and listenin' to them two swap lies. 'Course Will Rogers is kind of a western type fella too, ya know."

"They even look alike, same kind of open friendly faces."

"Yuh. Rogers was a little quieter man, I think, than Russell. He wasn't quite as forward. If Charlie Russell wanted to do something or say something, he done it and said it. Will Rogers didn't pull no punches, but he was a little slower in gettin' started."

Tom told me a small-world story. He was in Point Barrow, Alaska, with one of his sons and happened to meet the old Eskimo who was first to come across the small plane in which Will Rogers died. "He was pretty interested that I knew Rogers."

"So am I. I remember reading somewhere about the friendship between Russell and Rogers, and it was mentioned that Will Rogers, the great storyteller, let Charlie do most of the talking when they were together. He enjoyed his stories so much."

"I'll put it this way, I guess, [Russell] wasn't exactly a liar but he was kinda reckless with the truth. Paul liked stayin' with Charlie Russell. Paul liked tellin' stories, imagining things, Paul was quite a character, we all miss him, he died here about two years ago on the operating table. He was like old Russell, I got a kick out of him—if he didn't know a story he could figure one out. That's part of the deal—appreciating a good yarn. A long time ago if you hired out here the first of May, you wouldn't get back 'til the last of October. Unless ya sang a song yourself or told a story or somethin', that's all you'd ever see. Didn't have no TVs or radios or anything else, ya know. Kinda had to make your own amusement."

I offered, "Perhaps that's why so many early cowboys learned to draw. It seems every old book I come across written by a cowboy was illustrated by the author. Do you know any cowboy-artists besides Russell?"

"Bill, he was kinda an artist, my oldest brother. In fact, he was a good artist. Charlie got connected with Bill some way and he told him when you draw a picture, like say you draw a bucking horse out there, well, what caused the horse to buck? Put somethin' in the picture that caused it. A rabbit jumpin' outa the bush or a rattlesnake somewhere."

This is the realism old hands love. Kenny Trowbridge explained why.

"You take a guy nowdays—I bet J.K. Ralston'll tell you the same goddarned thing—take a guy who wants to be a painter and put him up agin of these old boys' paintings here and you're gonna see a helluva a lot of difference. Cuz his idea is comin' from someplace else, only way he's got to go back to somethin' in the past is to see a picture, get what I mean?"

"What about all this stuff western artists are doing right now?"

"It just ain't there, that's all," Kenny insisted. "I don't care how good the artist is, some old boy can take a look at it and say 'Hell, that ain't like it was at all.' There was a picture of a ranch with a bunch of white-faced cattle that hung down at the bank, and it was a nice picture, but it was nuthin' like it really was. Them big old white-faced cows, look like they've been grained for God only knows how long. For a western picture it just didn't set up at all."

My mind wandered into its western-romantic mode. I wondered if the creative spirit flourished more back in the old days. "J.K. told me he was first influenced by two schoolteachers, Miss Wheeler and Miss Stokes. He told me when you had art classes back in those days, everybody was an artist."

"Yuh, well," Kenny replied, "but they didn't all pan out by a helluva lot."

I dropped in on Tony Grace that same day to talk about western art. It may seem surprising that old cowhands are eager to talk about art and poetry, but it makes sense. As young working hands, they made heroes out of artists Charlie Russell and Will James, poets D.J. O'Malley and Robert Service.

Tony echoed Kenny's sentiment. "A man couldn't paint it if he hadn't lived it. Now [Frederic] Remington was a good painter, a good artist, but as far as his western stuff goes, to me it's phony. He got his ideas from the first cowhands that moved into the state, it's all Texas-style, didn't paint the true picture...I'd pass him up for Russell, Ralston. A little later than Russell, Will James depicted the way it was."

In 1984, when J.K. won the Montana Governor's Art Award, I told Tony about the festivities in Billings and showed him a print of a painting by J.K. Tony peered at it closely, "It's the arrival of the iron horse. The details are all there. The train must have whistled. See, the stagecoach horse is rearin' up." Tony's voice became even more enthusiastic, "Here's a cow runnin' with her tail up—the calf, he's spooked. That cow and calf are very good, they get spooked and throw their tails up just like that. And these two horses are spooked..."

"How can you tell?" I asked. Tony, ninety-four at the time, was awaiting cornea transplants, yet he caught details on a postcard-size print that I had missed upon seeing the original mural in the Great Northern Hotel in Billings.

"You can see the way they're leanin' over and both of 'em lookin' that way that they're spooked. The rider's lookin' that way, too." Tony was excited, his voice ringing out. He took one more close look. "The stage coach looks right. Last one I saw was in Winnemucca, Nevada in 1913, that's when I went out with Miller and Lux on that trail herd. Still one of those stagecoaches coming in from the north. Looked very much like this one in Ralston's painting. It looks like a Concord, but I don't know enough about stagecoaches to identify them from pictures, I don't even know how many makes there were."

Another time, looking at a print of Russell's painting "Bronc to Breakfast," Tony filled me in about it as well; he knew the picture—in fact, he knew the cowboy on the bucking bronco. "Doc Nelson was his name, he got on the bronc and that's what happened. The horse breaks in two. Russell was in camp at this time and witnessed the ride, and that inspired him to draw this painting. Doc Nelson was a man along in years when I met him, had quit bronc riding. I knew him real well, a man who had a sense of humor, fun to listen to. One time he and another puncher got their heads together and went around taking orders for saddle blankets, said they were made out of porcupine skins..."

As Tony peered at the small details of Russell's work, he wasn't sitting in his cozy living room, he was fifty miles outside Miles City again, sitting on the ground, watching as a wild bronc turned breakfast into chaos.

He had one criticism, and that was that Russell beautified the cowboys' features. "He was more realistic about the horses, wagons and scenery. A fella asked Russell one time where he got all the good-lookin' cowboys. In reality, some of the cowboys were actually homely as hell."

Kenny had made the same comment about Will James' cowboys, but he added that James' men all looked like the same man—even little kids looked like that man, only smaller. Tony agreed, "James used one man all the time, purty good-looking."

By looking at saddles in "Bronc to Breakfast," Tony could tell what part of the country the men were from and how they roped cows. "These are center-fire saddles, that's a saddle with a cinch right in the middle, come up from Texas, popular in the West during Russell's time. Russell's pictures are usually these center-fire men. Men with saddles like that used rawhide ropes and dallied when they roped, in other words they never tied to the saddle horn when they roped, they took a few turns which they called dallying."

"You know what, Tony? I could bring in a stack of Russell and Ralston prints and have you talk about them and I'd get the whole picture. Is J.K. precise, can you look at a Ralston painting and see where the cowboy came from?"

"Oh, yes," Tony replied, and using "Filly Chasers" as an example, he could tell from the rigging, spurs and hat that the subject was from eastern Montana. Peering closer, he said, "Now this is the way we carried our beds, no pack saddle, just folded your bed just right and laid it over the horse, the end would come way down sometimes..."

I recalled something J.K. had said, and passed it along to Tony. "'To those that have been there'," I quoted, "'the pictures talk back'."

Lying is a lost art.

Kenny Trowbridge

Kenny Trowbridge spellbinds a St. Louis audience in 1982 with his tall tales. Photo by Jo Rainbolt

Baldfaced Liars

Cowboys loved horses, women, biscuits, beefsteak and bald-faced lies. A man who could spin a "big windy" was valued around the campfire. Not every cowpoke had the gift of exaggeration.

Tom Harwood said "part of the deal" of being a cowboy was appreciating a good yarn. Working miles away from town for months at a time required self-amusement. My long-time friends—Joe Hughes, Art Wahl, Tony Grace, J.K. Ralston—told great stories but they told things exactly as they happened. When I was looking for a master at big windies, luck led me to Kenny Trowbridge.

One of the first things Kenny told me when I visited him and his wife Verna in their bungalow in Darby was that lying is a lost art. "There seems to be more of 'em, but liars are all amateurs these days," he lamented. Kenny's booming voice, and his tall tales and outlandish stories reflected what the cowhand loved best—the ability to laugh at life. Such wit is a built-in reaction among all the old cowhands. Joe was a stickler with facts; he whittled the truth to bare bones. But he was playful about it. At the least, he made a wry comment after telling a serious story. To cowboys, all subjects deserve an occasional dose of humor.

"What you doin' in town?" my elderly Indian pal Louie Gingras asked on a grim day in the early 1970s.

"Funeral. Art Evans died," I replied with great sadness. Art never worked as a cowhand, he owned the best book store in Missoula, Montana, and collected rare books and rare people. He met Louie through me, and treasured my "Louie stories." Art was seventy when he died; Louie had already outlived him by a decade.

Louie chuckled, "Art died, huh? Funny, he never done that before."

Like many Indians, Louie had worked as a cowhand as a young fellow; he was even nicknamed "Cowboy." Cowboys can be quite sentimental about death, but Louie could see I needed to lighten up. It worked. After a moment of disbelief, I laughed, realizing how much Art would have appreciated the comment. The funeral didn't do it, but Louie's comment brought Art back.

Range humor isn't farfetched. It grew from everyday occurrences. Living close to nature gave the cowhand plenty of raw material. Not surprisingly, a major theme was weather. "Usta git a helluva lot colder," Kenny stated once when Louie and I visited. "One wintertime we filled the bunkhouse stove up with a buncha wood, it was so cold the flames froze. The wind broke 'em off, they landed over by the fence. Thawed out in the spring and set the place on fire."

If Kenny had been sitting around the campfire or bunkhouse, another hand would have taken up the challenge with a colder-than-cold anecdote. But this was a solo performance in the Trowbridges' kitchen, where ninety-year-old Louie dozed by the woodstove. Kenny went on, "Another time we was settin' around the woodstove wondering how cold it was outside. No way to tell, so we put a bucket full of water on the woodstove and ran outside with it. It was still boilin' when we thawed it out, it froze that quick."

Kenny told true stories, too. "One time in Wyoming it was too windy to set up a tent. I walked around the side of a building and saw an old guy settin' there and said, 'Dad, does it blow this way all the time?' He said, 'No, son, it blows the other way part of the time'."

I egged Kenny on. "How about hot weather, a cowboy told me about the time it got so hot the corn all popped..."

"Oh yuh," Kenny replied, "and the cattle seen it, thought it was snow and froze to death."

That's the way it went. Another familiar theme was critters. Cowhands respect animals, and their stories play up "human" characteristics, with animals proving to be smarter, nicer, humbler (more human!). The amazing "dawgs" of Kenny's boyhood acted quickly and victoriously in dangerous situations, then went back to being obedient creatures without a bragging word.

"Remember me tellin' you about Old Major being able to read? Did I ever tell ya about the time we sold that cow..." and Kenny related how Major kept circling farther and farther away from the ranch, trying to bring in the missing cow. The poor dog wore himself out and wouldn't give up until Ken's dad showed him the bill of sale.

Some of Kenny's best stories are take-offs on his family. Old Granddad who collected hound dogs and wore shoes only twice—once when he married Grandma and again when the undertaker got him. Granddad owned every breed of hound dog and when he saw a pointer from the South he figured it was a hound he hadn't seen and convinced the owner to let him take the dog for a trial hunt. When he returned the pointer, he gave this critique, "The dawg's got a good nose, he never barks, and every so often he stops and puts one foot kinda in front of the other and his tail gets stiff as a board. But I broke him of that."

Other topics ready-made for cowhand humor included: law and order, chuck wagon cooks, greenhorns, Englishmen and preachers. Kenny tells a story that took place on a Sunday morning: "Cars were just in, and this cowpoke was all over the road driving home to the ranch. He'd had too much to drink after a Saturday night out and was purty wobbly. There was a preacher behind him tryin' to get to a little country church. That ol' cowboy was back and forth, the preacher just couldn't pass, finally there was a wide place in the road and the preacher gunned around him. Trouble is he went too far to the side and

On New Year's Day 1992, Tony Grace makes sure the author understands his point—as did all of the old cowhands interviewed for this book, whether the story of the moment was tall or true. Photo by Lee Zimmerman

drove over the bank. The cowboy got out of his car. 'You hurt?' 'No, I'm not hurt, I got the Lord ridin' with me,' the preacher replied. 'Better let him ride with me,' the cowboy said, 'the way you drive you'll kill him'."

Kenny's career as a nationally-acclaimed storyteller began quietly. I drove him and his wife, Verna, to the University of Montana and, while Verna toured the campus (she'd heard his stories ten thousand times), Kenny entertained students in a class taught by Michael Korn. Kenny told things straight that night. Much to his surprise, the students were an appreciative audience and asked numerous questions about earlier days in the West. On the sixty-mile drive home, Kenny told more stories, and even sang some old Irish ballads. Every so often he'd take off his cowboy hat, scratch his full head of hair and, sounding pleased, he'd mutter, "I cain't believe it, college students, fer Crissake, and they were interested in the way it was."

In the spring of 1982, he braved a 707 jet to participate in a national storytelling event in St. Louis, Missouri. Kenny had never flown, the farthest he'd been from western Montana was the 500 miles to Seattle when he trucked a load of cattle there in the 1940s.

It was Verna who coaxed me into going along on the St. Louis trip. She wanted someone to sit with Kenny on the plane so she could talk to people. She may have panicked at the idea of speaking in front of a group, but Verna never knew a stranger.

The author's viewpoint of Jake Chanate and Kenny Trowbridge on during their 1982 radio interview in St. Louis. Photo by Jo Rainbolt

Kenny paled as we boarded the plane, but he was still up to an apt comparison—"Jes' like a goldurned cattle-dipping vat," he mumbled. As we circled St. Louis, he looked down at the city, "Lord, look at that, will ya? I guess if they really want me, I'm glad I'm going, but what'll I tell all them people?"

Kenny just talked, and the crowds loved it. Mostly he told stories about old hands he knew as a boy in the Lemhi Valley of Idaho. "I was the kid then, and I'm still the kid," Kenny once said, referring to the age difference between himself and two other Bitterroot Valley cowboys—Joe Hughes and Tony Grace. Kenny hadn't lived as close to the open range era as Tony and Joe did. I usually didn't listen much to cowboys under age eighty, but hearing Kenny's stories made me realize how much I needed his viewpoint. He appreciated the early West of his boyhood, knowing it was on the way out. The old-time hands lived it, Kenny embraced it. He became an interpreter who spoke the language of another era.

In St. Louis, Kenny told most of his stories in front of a covered wagon or in the chuck wagon display at the huge Jefferson National Expansion Memorial Museum along the Mississippi River. The underground museum's circular design, with softly lit displays and carpeted steps, made it an ideal setting for storytelling. Kids gathered around Kenny and asked about his cowboy boots, his tall hat with the rattlesnake band, his grizzly claw necklace. Adults sprawled comfortably on the wide carpeted steps and howled when Kenny told tales about wagon wheels swelling up from rattlesnake bites, and dawgs riding on running boards and retrieving duck-swallowing fish.

"That old guy's real—he's been there," an onlooker observed. Kenny was compared to Will Rogers and to an old-time cowhand on a teLevi'sion commercial. After one presentation, a well-dressed gentleman approached me (I'd been roped into introducing Kenny, and often acted as his straight-man) and said he could make a Hollywood celebrity of Kenny. I smiled and told him Kenny didn't like to fly, that planes reminded him of cattle-dipping vats.

Kenny was a natural, and each day it became more apparent. He knew how to hold a crowd and when to deliver the punch line. His voice and inflection were perfect. He was often asked how he became a professional storyteller, and he talked about Michael Korn, "one of them folklorists," inviting him to a university class. "That was a year ago. I sorta thought it was a buncha hooey but I went and I realized these people—twenty, maybe thirty years old—don't know what things were really like. And it's gettin' away. If we who lived it don't talk about it, it's gonna run plumb out."

Kenny teamed up with Jake Chanate, a Kiowa Indian who told Trickster tales learned from his grandmother. They were a hilarious match, not only in wit, but also in ample-belly builds. Kenny referred to his Indian partner as "War Whoop." When asked about the stagecoach the two were standing in front of, Jake replied, "I dunno nuthin' about it. You'll have to ask my cowboy friend here, we just chased these things."

Kenny and Jake appeared on radio and teLevi'sion together, and were a highlight at the "swapping ground," where they informally exchanged cowboy and Indian stories. During the grand finale performance, they were being taped for teLevi'sion. Because each could carry on forever, I was given the job of signaling from a front row when time was running out. I was told to be discreet, but Jake kept glancing my way and asking, "How we doin', Jo?"

"Time runnin' low yet?" "Whaddaya say, Boss?" He was getting back at me for making faces at him when he had been interviewed on radio.

Another character at the event was rodeo cowboy and Arkansas rancher Glenn Ohrlin, author of a cowboy songbook, *The Hellbound Train,* and a popular performer at folk festivals and on college campuses. Glenn parked his bedroll in the same home where Verna, Kenny and I were put up. I became the lucky onlooker in a late night popcorn-munching, lie-swapping, song-exchanging session. Kenny, new to the national network of cowboy song singers and story tellers, had a motherlode of original material. Glenn, a born collector of cowboy lore, was delighted with the new stuff.

One of the songs Glenn sang that night was "Boomer Johnson," the story of one hand's retribution against a murderous cook given to such actions as punching his six-shooter through rock-hard doughnuts and into a cowhand's belly while saying, "Yer eatin' some." When Glenn and Kenny later joined other cowhands on a national "Old Punchers Reunion" sponsored by the National Council for the Traditional Arts, I saw grown men and women hold their sides and weep at Kenny's rendition of "Boomer."

"Boomer" became Kenny's personal favorite. Glenn, on the other hand, was delighted to be introduced to the poem "Reincarnation," written by eastern Montana rancher Wally MacRae, tracing how a cowhand, through a series of transformations, could continue existence as a cowpie.

Lack of professional jealousy among cowboy-entertainers is impressive. Songs, stories and poems are out of a cowboy's mouth and into circulation. A lot of song and poem rustling went on in the past, but if Glenn and Kenny are any example, modern poets and storytellers go to great lengths to credit the author. Poems are memorized with impressive ease. Kenny could not remember names (except, of course, horses'), but no one picked up a poem quicker. Like Joe Hughes and a lot of old hands, Kenny started memorizing poems as a kid. Schooling wasn't necessary, memorization was. But Kenny never dreamed he'd be called upon to recite those poems and embellish those stories fifty years later.

Kenny and Verna were taken aback by the traffic and crowds in St. Louis. When Kenny was told that the storytelling event and accompanying Charlie Russell exhibition drew more than 7,000 people, he replied, "I thought I saw more people than that in that damn traffic jam after the Cardinals' ball game."

After that first event, Kenny attended many more. He was out of his armchair, answering the phone and going for the mail, but he was unchanged. He couldn't quite believe there was an audience for stuff he grew up with.

"Doggarn poems and stuff, ya know, when I was a kid, they never got away much. It just went with the outfit. Then when somebody'd go from that outfit over to another outfit and they was tellin' stories or singin' songs, you'd have a new one, see. They didn't go around writin' these doggone things down or publishing 'em or stuff like they do nowdays. It's still kinda odd to me that ya just told a story in my day and, by Jesus, now they're willin' to listen to it."

Wilf Carter, in stage-cowboy getup in the 1930s, billed himself as the "Yodeling Cowboy" before he became "Montana Slim." Courtesy of Jeanette Ziesemer

Too many dead cowboys.

Joe Hughes, on cowboy songs

The Cowpoke's Songbag

Cow camp culture comes alive in cowboy songs. They tell the whole story; all the listener needs to do is pay attention to the words. Printed neatly on the neck of Glenn Ohrlin's guitar is an endless list of songs. It's Glenn's songbag, he knows the words and melodies to all of them. When he comes across a new song that strikes his fancy, into the songbag it goes.

Feeling nostalgic? It's hard to match the nostalgia an oldtimer has for the open range days. Listen to the first lines of one of Glenn's songs, "Make Me a Cowboy Again":

Backward, turn backward, O Time, with your wheels,
Aeroplanes, wagons and automobiles.
Dress me once more in sombrero that flaps,
Spurs and a flannel shirt, slicker and chaps...

And the last line pleads,

Make me a cowboy again for one day.

Cowboy songs made the rounds quicker than a runaway bronc, so it's not easy to track down composers. Glenn said the sentimental "Backward, Turn Backward, O Time in Your Flight" has been a familiar song since before the turn of the century and that George B. German from South Dakota credits the cowboy adaptation to brothers named Joe and Zack Miller, who performed in a Wild West show.

But, Glenn said, writers are overly keen to remark on the sadness of cowboy songs. "Seems to me a lot more are comical," drawled the Arkansas cowboy with the poker face. He certainly has some funny songs in his personal songbag. such as the wryly rendered "The Gol-Darned Wheel."

The song documents the introduction of a bronc buster to a bicycle. The cowboy is a braggart:

> *I can ride the wildest bronco in the wild and woolly West,*
> *I can rake him, I can break him, let him do his level best.*
> *I can handle any cattle ever wore a coat of hair,*
> *And I've had a lively tussle with a tarnal grizzly bear.*

The other hands decide the fellow is bragging too much and challenge him to straddle the "wheel," a bicycle tied outside the ranch house by a visiting tenderfoot. The bronc buster manages to mount the contraption, then proceeds to fly downslope toward the creek, the wheel not only "gallyflutin' like lightning, but whizzing and dartin' and wobbling like a bat." Nothing the hand tries can stop it.

> *I pulled up on the handles but I couldn't check it up,*
> *I yanked and sawed and hollered, but the darn thing wouldn't stop.*
> *And then a sort of meechin' in my brain began to steal*
> *That the devil had a mortgage on that gol-darned wheel.*

The hand's last conscious thought is of a spinning world and tangled stars, until he finds himself lying in the bunkhouse with the boys gathered around.

> *And a doctor was a-sewing on the skin where it was ripped,*
> *And Old Arizona whispered, "Well, old boy, I guess you're whipped."*
> *I said that "I am busted from sombrero down to heel."*
> *He grinned and said, "You ort to see that gol-darned wheel!"*

Kenny Trowbridge was another cowboy with an impressive collection in his personal songbag. Storyteller Kenny sang with ease and gusto, just as he talked. With these two punchers as friends, I've heard some rare old songs.

I first heard Kenny sing the classic "Zebra Dun" while sitting at his kitchen table. No guitar or banjo, not even a harmonica, just Kenny and his Irish tenor. It's a great song. The fellows in it are "camped out on the plains at the head of the Cimarron, when along came a stranger and he stopped to argue some."

In western fashion, the hands in the song serve breakfast to the duded-up stranger, who immediately begins to talk about the world and politics. The fourth verse goes:

> *Such an educated feller, his thoughts just come in herds.*
> *He astonished all the cowboys with his jaw-breakin' words.*
> *He just kept right on a-talkin' till he made the boys all sick.*
> *Then we began to look around just how to play a trick.*

The chance for fun comes when the stranger said he was on his way to a riding job and asks to borrow a "nice fat saddle hoss." The hands laugh up their sleeves and rope old Zebra Dun, an outlaw who'd "paw the white out of the moon."

There's a wealth of wild-ride descriptions in cowboy songs, but the three verses describing the dude on Zebra Dun are my favorite:

When the stranger hit the saddle old Dunny quit the earth
And he traveled right straight up for all that he was worth.
A-pitchin' and a-squealin' and a-havin' wall-eyed fits,
His hind feet perpendicular, the front ones in the bits.

You could see the tops of the mountains under Dunny every jump,
But the stranger he just sat there just like a camel's hump.
The stranger sat upon him and twirled his black moustache
Just like a summer boarder a-waitin' for his hash.

He thumped him in the shoulders and spurred him when he whirled
To show them flunkly punchers he was the wolf of the world.
And when he had dismounted, once more upon the ground,
We knowed he was a Thoroughbred and not a gent from town.

The boss offers the stranger a job, "If you can throw a lasso like you rode old Zebra Dun, you're the man I've been a-looking for since the year of one."

The song ends with this revelation: "There's one thing and a sure thing I've learned since I was born, every educated fellow ain't a plumb greenhorn!"

Kenny said it was common for well-dressed strangers to turn out to be top riders. Sometimes the greenhorn was actually a top bronc buster dressed for fun. Glenn sang "Zebra Dun," too, and he related stories about two top rodeo riders who enjoyed pulling the gag. "A great bronc rider of the Thirties, Johnny Slater, would show up at the rodeo in tweeds and cloth cap, smoking a pipe. When his turn came around, they found he could write his name on a really rank bucking horse."

The other trickster, Paddy Ryan, was a well-known horse-raiser in Montana and a money-winning contest rider in the 1920s and 1930s. Glenn heard a story in which Paddy showed up at a big cow outfit in Nevada, dressed in a cloth cap and pinchback coat and city shoes, to ride the rough string. Glenn said all the boys were howling to themselves until they saw old Paddy ride.

Perhaps the best-known cowboy song of all is "Strawberry Roan." For a change, there's no doubt as to the songwriter. Bronc rider Curley Fletcher wrote it around 1915. In "Strawberry Roan," a bronc peeler who claims "the bronc never lived that I couldn't fan," meets his match in "...the worst bucker I seen on the range, he can turn on a nickel and give you some change."

The bronc goes up so high he leaves the cowboy "a-settin' up there in the sky."

The song ends with a new-found humility and a challenge to other bronc peelers:

> Then I know there's old ponies I ain't able to ride.
> There's some of them livin', they haven't all died.
> But I bet all my money the man ain't alive
> Can ride old Strawberry when he makes his high dive.

Such a song inspired sequels and parodies. Glenn did a good job of tracking them down, including some he called too salty to print, such as Fletcher's "Castration of the Strawberry Roan." Kenny Trowbridge recalled verses from a song documenting a gentler taming of the roan—in which a sweet schoolmarm subdued the unrideable cayuse.

At least two of the more memorable versions came out of Canada, written by wrangler-singer Wilf "Montana Slim" Carter, who was still performing and recording at age 87 in 1991. The first version features Harry Knight, a top bronc rodeo rider from the Canadian Rockies in the 1920s and '30s who, legend had it, actually rode the roan. It's called, appropriately, "He Rode the Strawberry Roan." In the second song, "The Fate of the Strawberry Roan," the crusty horse hangs up on a corral after one of his legendary high dives and has to be shot. He is given a proper burial, with his grave-marker signed by all the hands he's thrown and his saddle propped over it.

In 1982, I had the chance to round up a lot of old songs, poems and stories when I co-produced a record for the Montana Folk Life Project, "When the Work's All Done This Fall." Director Michael Korn didn't hire me for my musical ability but because of my network of old cowboy friends.

Tracking down songs was fun. We wanted men who grew up in the ranch tradition, fellows who learned "Strawberry Roan" from Aunt Sue or the hired hand.

"Know any singers of old cowboy songs?" I asked a maid in a Miles City motel. Mike and I had driven twelve hours straight across wide Montana to real cow country. The maid knew Louis Schlautman, dairy farmer by day ("They're still cows."), electric guitar bar-singer by night. Dim the lights, hand him a guitar, and Lou will sing the prettiest, most tear-wrenching version I've ever heard of "Little Joe the Wrangler."

One of the most popular cowboy songs, "Little Joe" is about a kid "with broken shoes and overalls," who runs away from a mean stepmother and whose dream comes true one stormy night when he is allowed to help with a stampede. Little Joe is trampled to death. Cowhands like the song; their preference runs to songs that are outright spoofs or that tell stories that ring true, no matter how sentimental the theme.

As if "Little Joe" wasn't sad enough, Glenn knew a version "Little Joe the

Wrangler's Sister Nell" that has "a slender little figure dressed in gray" ride into camp looking for her brother the day after the stampede.

While on the trail for cowboy songs, I heard about Paul Young. Paul lived in a retirement apartment complex in Miles City. I rushed in and introduced myself, eager to whisk Paul away to a recording session with Mike.

"Pleased to meet you, but don't take another step," were Paul's first words.

I obeyed but asked why.

"I just dropped one of my hearing aids. It's tiny, but if neither of us move we might find it."

I spotted it immediately, perched on the red shag carpet of Paul's western-inspired bachelor apartment.

"Oh, boy, do I thank you. You're my friend for life."

I was, too. Although Paul, born in 1892, lived only a few years longer and I never saw him again after that evening, his letters arrived regularly during those remaining years.

Like all the hands of his generation, Paul had gotten around. When I met him in 1982, he was a slight wisp of a man who needed a cane, two hearing aides and bottle-glass bifocals to navigate. But I had learned long before that, where old cowboys are concerned, appearances mean nothing.

Raised in the Wasatch Mountains in Utah by a mother who wanted her bright son to be a civil engineer, Paul became hooked on horses when he broke his first bronc at age thirteen. By the time he was eighteen, he'd cowboyed his way to Montana.

During a taping session that lasted until midnight, Paul would break into song while describing trail drives of the generation of cowboys who proceeded him. His voice was hearty and robust, not the voice of a frail man nearing ninety. He was tireless. "Come a ky-yi-yippie, yippie-yea, yippie-yea," he sang, and explained that this oldest trail song—"Old Chisholm Trail"—had a verse for every state between Montana and Texas. He knew most of them and somehow stretched the singing-talking history lesson way back to Mexico in the 1500s when, he said, Queen Isabella of Spain sent a thousand horses to the New World.

Paul appeared to know all the old songs and, when he forgot a stanza, he created his own. Typical of a lot of old hands, he considered trail songs his favorite.

"You can always tell a trail song, it has a lilt, sort of a feeling like you're on horseback. The rhythm goes with the riding," Paul explained. Then he deflated the myth of the Hollywood-style drive, "Trailing cattle wasn't fast, you can push 'em along, but easy."

After he got married in Miles City, Paul bought an ice business in Terry, on the plains of eastern Montana. "They always say you need a strong back and a weak mind to be a cowboy and that proved it. I bought that business just before Frigidaire came in." He did better on his first ranch—paying twenty cents an acre for land on the north side of the Yellowstone River and forty cents for southside land.

Old punchers like Paul prefer songs made up by men like themselves. If a man hadn't been there, the song didn't work quite right. D.J. "Kid White" O'Malley was a top Montana hand in the 1880s and 1890s, and his songs and poems reflect the humor and spirit of the open range days. There's no doubt about Kid White's having been there. He was ten in 1877 when the family moved to Fort Keogh on the Yellowstone River in Montana where his soldier stepfather was stationed. Kid White began his cowboy career as a horse wrangler at age fourteen to help support his mother and sisters after his stepfather disappeared.

O'Malley got little credit for his songs during his lifetime, even though much of his work was printed in the *Montana Stockgrowers Journal*, published weekly in Miles City. That's where his classic "When the Work's All Done This Fall" first appeared October 6, 1893 under the title, "The Last Roundup." Only old hands, cowboy-song buffs and folklorists know about the song these days, but it was popular in O'Malley's youthful days and stayed that way for a while—a 78 r.p.m. record that came out almost thirty years after O'Malley wrote it sold 900,000 copies! It wasn't copyrighted so I doubt if O'Malley earned a penny.

The ballad described death during a roundup. It began:

A group of jolly cowboys
Discussed their plans at ease,
Said one: I'll tell you something
Boys, if you please:
See, I'm a puncher,
Dressed most in rags,
I used to be a wild one
And took on big jags.

The puncher goes on in the song to talk about his home, "…a good one, you know," and his intention to visit home and Mother and set things right "when work is done this fall."

That night during a stampede, his horse stumbles and crushes him. As he lies dying, he says:

"Bill, take my saddle,
George, take my bed,

Fred take my pistol
After I am dead.
Think of me kindly
When on them you look—"
His voice then grew fainter,
With anguish he shook.

The last stanza uttered by O'Malley's dying cowboy ends:

He uttered a few words,
Heard by them all:
"I'll see my mother
When work's done this fall."

When folklorist Mike Korn and I recorded Bitterroot Valley rancher Earsel "Swede" Bloxham, he sang this song with an extra verse that an anonymous poet tagged on and that is widely used:

Poor Charlie was buried at sunrise,
No tombstone on his head,
Nothing but a little board and this is what it said,
"Charlie died at daybreak, he died from a fall,
And he'll not see his mother
When the work's all done this fall."

Earsel sang the old songs straight from his heart. He was seventy and looked fifty, wore a Gene-Autry-style felt and had the kindest face I've ever seen. He sang with a twang, a downhome sound that always made me teary. But that effect wasn't universal. After a moving rendition by Earsel of "There's an Empty Cot in the Bunkhouse Tonight" at a folk day event in the Bitterroot Valley, old Joe Hughes turned to me and said, "Too many dead cowboys."

The comment made me laugh, for it was prime Joe, who disliked anything that sentimentalized the cowboy.

A discussion on cowboy songs would not be complete without mention of punchers singing on night guard. There's been considerable debate about whether or not cowhands sang during the tiring two-hour night guard. All the old hands I've talked to say, yup, it kept them awake and also lulled the cattle. J.K. Ralston said, "You had to do something, a man would go crazy talking to himself for two hours."

J.K. added that it wasn't like movies portray, with some fella croonin' away in the moonlight up on a ridge, watching the cattle. "We were right there, circling the cattle. Singing kept the cows from hearing twigs snapping and other spooky night noises. It wasn't exactly singing, it sounded more like 'ba-booon, ba-boon'."

Tony Grace on his horse Rex, overlooking his summer range from Horse Butte outside of West Yellowstone, Montana. Tony recalled that Rex, a roping horse, had a way of dropping his head and shaking it, as if in disgust, when Tony missed a throw. Courtesy of Stan Grace

Epilogue

In the mid-1980s, in the midst of researching this book, I was fond of saying that old cowhands live forever. After all, Joe Hughes was still alive, years since his doctor had taken me aside during one of Joe's bouts in the hospital and told me I was going to lose my old friend.

Joe's heart was shot—the doctor described it as "more like a sponge than a muscle"—and he also suffered from emphysema, stomach and prostate problems. Between spells in the hospital, Joe would convince his doctor he could manage on his own, his one-room bachelor apartment across from the copper-domed Ravalli County Museum (Hamilton's old court house). Not that poor health was fun. His broad shoulders sloped; the flesh on his upper arms became, in his words, "loose as elephant hide," his movie star features sharpened to the bone—he said he looked like an old turkey.

I stepped into his hospital room one bright fall afternoon and found him in a coughing frenzy. He didn't see me standing at the door. My first thought was to turn around; after all, I reasoned, would Irish Joe want me to see him in such a pathetic state? But I went forward to give the old cowhand some help. After he recovered a bit, Joe cocked a bushy eyebrow up at me, "Sure beats the conceit out of a guy."

Joe claimed the perplexity of poor health was this—it kept his mind too much on himself. One day while feeling particularly miserable, he recalled a poem that addressed the subject. Two of the five verses went like this:

Figger up your blessings
Instead of always finding fault
And lookin' as dejected
As a sick cow lickin' salt.

Ain't it better to be living
Right side up to take the knocks
Than to be carted to the boneyard
In a silver-handled box?

The night before Joe died in 1984, I was in a hurry. I dashed into his hospital room at Marcus Daly Memorial Hospital in Hamilton and commented on how well he looked, telling him I had to visit another old friend incarcerated down the hall, and I was ready to dash back out when he stopped me with a story about the priest who had visited that day. Joe had heard him pause behind the partition and said, "Father, I'll take a shot from that flask."

The incident stopped me at the foot of Joe's bed. I grinned, and the last words I recall hearing from Joe were that that's what he wanted: to see me smile.

Kenny Trowbridge had commented that Joe beat the odds and kept on living because he never scared himself to death. "Everybody gets het up when they get real sick. Joe just don't give a damn. He'll go when it's time, he ain't about to be worried into dying."

Kenny's time came relatively early. His wife Verna said the two of them walked home from the Darby Senior Citizen's noon meal at Bud and Shirley's Cafe and, the next thing she knew, she looked out the window and he'd keeled over in the back yard. This youngster of the old cowhands died August 28, 1989, the day after his 77th birthday. Tony Grace, 99 at the time, hadn't expected to outlive his best pal.

During Kenny's funeral in Hamilton, the sound of a fiddle came from behind a screen. I knew the unseen musician playing his heart out was champion fiddler Jimmy Widner, a retired millwright from Darby. Jimmy played the old cowboy songs—the ones that caused Kenny to bawl out "Now thar's a real one!" and I cried the tears I hadn't shed over Joe's death. Norwegians have a hard time crying, even at funerals, but as Jimmy kept playing the old tunes, I continued crying. I cried because Kenny was gone—Kenny with his gentleness and crazy humor and outrage at modern foolishness—and I cried some more because Tony, who was sitting next to me, would die and who would take their place?

A wheelchair had been provided for Tony. When I wheeled him to the casket at the end of the service, he peered at Kenny's face for what seemed like a long time, then saluted him. I cried some more. Good work for a Norwegian.

My old cowhands were not going to live forever. Most of them would not see this book come to print.

Tony, age 101, and Donovan McGee, 83, are the only main characters in this book who have seen it to completion. When I called Don in Juneau late in 1991, he chalked up his good health to "just lucky," although he said living outside most of his life probably had something to do with it. An old Norwegian that Don had been caring for, in much the same style as the early cowhands took care of each other, had just died. "He had quite a history, born in 1902, jumped ship from Norway at 16 and landed in Alaska, married two or three times," Don said over the phone. "Cantankerous old fellow. Took out Social Security and everything, but never became a citizen." I told Don I was glad he looked after him, to which he replied, "Somebody has to do it."

The laconic Art Wahl seemed to get more talkative as he got older. Since

I'd moved to Missoula, I could drop in on him at the Oxford, a downtown workingman's bar with brains and eggs on the menu, open twenty-four hours a day (legend says it has never been locked). Art always seemed willing to put down his cards and visit. He said a man could only play so much poker and, those days, he was playing for want of something else to do. While we talked, the fellow behind the counter would fix Art's supper, a hamburger on whole wheat bread (not a bun).

"Did you know any dumb horses?" I asked Art one late afternoon over my barley soup.

"Dumb?" he chuckled. "Ya. Lotsa those, learn 'em to work and that's all."

We sat in silence. I spooned in barley soup. "Work, eh?" I finally put in.

"Work. Ya," Art replied. "I couldn't go to town [Miles City] without, 'When ya gonna work for me?' I could outwork anybody. I put in some long days."

Another silence. I spooned in more soup. I grew up with a Norwegian for a father, I know when something is brewing. There's an inward look, a soft gleam of remembrance, that tells me to sit quietly if I want to hear more. It was late November, a time when the Missoula Valley closes in. Snow turns to drizzle, the voice on the local radio warns that an air pollution alert is on. The Oxford, where street people rub elbows with an occasional college professor, and college football players play poker with old sheepherders, felt warm and safe.

"I have trouble sleeping," Art went on. "I go three or four days without sleep."

"What do you do at night, read?"

"Just lay there and rest. Daydream. Think about something, one thing after another comes up. Everything comes up. Something happens when I was a kid, something happens yesterday, something about the poker game."

And that gray Missoula afternoon in the steamy smoke-filled Oxford, Art told me how, before he left alone for the United States at age fourteen, he took a trip all over Norway as a kid, traveling with his school's chorale.

My silent old friend, a boy tenor. Imagine that.

Not too much after that visit, Art went into a nursing home. He'd been living with his daughter and son-in-law but it became too difficult when he awoke at all hours wanting to go to the Oxford. He got out of the home for a day when "the Ox" hosted an all-day drop-in party for his ninety-seventh birthday in December 1988. A huge cake, punch, cookies and old-time music were served up in the cavernous card room. The staff gave Art a soft wool cardigan and a poke of betting money. A bouncy "playboy bunny" tied balloons to the wheelchair the nursing home had provided and sang and danced a rousing rendition of "Happy Birthday." Art shook her hand.

Art had been in the home only a few weeks, and this was his first (and last) visit to the bar from there. "I'm not going back to that nursing home," he told me when the end of the party was drawing near. He sat in the wheelchair, a big, loose-jointed man with large expressive hands. "Why can't I just come to the Ox?"

Early that winter, Art was transferred from the nursing home to the Veteran's Home in Columbia Falls (up north near Glacier Park). He didn't know me the day I visited, nor did he recall the Ox or playing poker. Still, I was glad to see him. His silence was nothing new and his kindness was still written all over his face. The nurse assured me he was having a bad day and that on good days he remembered everything. Shortly before he died in the spring of 1991, he complained to his daughter Astrid that his memory was shot. "Well, you'll be a hundred years old your next birthday," she told him.

"Oh, well," Art replied. "If I'm that old I can forget anything I want to."

J.K. Ralston, a widower after 1974, didn't go downhill when he finally moved to institutionalized care. He warmed to it. I like to think of J.K. looking at it as experience, the same only different, as he had seen all the other things life presented to him. J.K. moved from his home in Billings with the log studio in the back yard to the home where he spent his last few years peacefully. J.K., like all natural storytellers, appreciated an audience. His daughter Marjorie Walter said that whenever she visited she found him surrounded by listeners.

I drove to Hamilton to take Tony Grace to lunch near the end of 1991, as this book approached press. At 101, his eyes and hearing were going, so he couldn't bach it like he'd hoped to do when Viola died the year before, but he was content in the retirement home he chose. "The only complaint I have, and it's minor," he told me over his dinner of chicken-fried steak, "is this," and he waved his fork over the food. He explained that the meals at the retirement home tended to be short on beef, but added that was understandable since all the residents on his floor except for him and one other fellow were women, who probably never had the need for much beef.

Although it frustrated him when he couldn't recall a name from 1909, and he claimed he was "losing his memory," Tony was as sharp as ever. He explained the efficiency of the retirement center's laundry system, we discussed the comfort level of underwear (it was the first wintry day after an extended Indian summer) and he wanted to hear all the details of a fall trip I had taken to Wisconsin.

Tony had proofed a draft of this book about four years earlier when I returned from rewriting it in Alaska, during the time he nicknamed me "Gypsy Jo" and even made up a poem about my travels all the way from "the Yu-catan to Juneau…you know." He admonished me to watch my descriptions. "Study how a horse rolls—study anything you want to describe, and then say it without fancy terms, in plain English."

When Tom Harwood's daughter Carma Adamson (the cowhand of the family) told me over the telephone that her father had been sick with pneumonia and died of cancer, I expressed sympathy at such a sad end for a man as unbeatable as Tom.

"He died well," she replied. "Kept active and had all his faculties until the end. He was full of cancer, even had it in his brain, but he didn't know it."

This sounded so much like the old cowhands.

Tom was hospitalized in Cut Bank with pneumonia in the late fall of 1988. "He wanted to get out for Christmas, he just couldn't miss the fiddlers' Christmas party, so the doctor let him out," Carma said. "He danced that night, had a wonderful time, played his fiddle so pretty; better, I think, than I've ever heard him."

Carma said her father seemed to be getting along fine, but in January he became ill and the doctor sent him to Conrad for tests. Upon learning the extent of Tom's cancer, the doctor asked him if he wanted to go on life support and Tom said, 'Hell no, my time to go, I'll go.' He was gone in two weeks.

Carma was with her dad when he died. The last thing he did was agree that a vanilla milkshake, his favorite, would hit the spot. The nurse suggested he rest until one of his kids returned with the shake. "That sounds like a good idea," Tom replied.

"He put his head down on the pillow and closed his eyes, and that was it," Carma said.

Carma said no one who knew Tom was surprised that he played and danced all night at a fiddlers' Christmas party and was gone a month later.

Index

Jo Rainbolt, author of An Elephant in Every Yard, *also about old-timers, lives in Missoula, Montana. She was a newspaperwoman based in Ravalli County in Montana's Bitterroot Valley for 10 years. A Wisconsin native, she moved to Montana to attend college in 1964 and stayed permanently. She collected oral histories for* The Last Cowboy *over a decade of friendships with old cowhands, and was anthropologist Michael Korn's partner in gathering cowboy songs for the recording "When the Work's All Done This Fall," produced by the Montana Folklife Project of the Montana Arts Council.*

Richard B. Roeder is professor emeritus in the department of history, Montana State University, Bozeman. He co-authored Montana: A History of Two Centuries *(University of Washington Press, 1976; rev. ed. 1990) and served on the editorial board for* The Last Best Place: A Montana Anthology *(Montana Historical Society Press, 1988).*